I0108906

SHE FOUND IT

IN

THE CLOUDS

Share a girl's exciting and dramatic journey...
filled with unending adventure, heartwarming inspiration
and destiny

By

Sharon M. Jones

© 2007 Sharon M. Jones
All rights reserved. No part of this publication may be reproduced or transmitted in
any form or by any means electronic or mechanical, including photocopy,
recording, or any information storage and retrieval system, without permission in
writing from both the copyright owner and the publisher.

Requests for permission to make copies of any part of this work should be mailed
to Permissions Department, Witty Writings Publishing, LLC, 2875-F Northtowne
Ln #232, Reno, NV. 89512

ISBN: 978-1-4276-1905-1

Printed in the United States of America by Witty Writings Press

Acknowledgements

I dedicate this gift to....

God; who created me simply for this purpose. I thank you for shaping me and taking me from the safety of my mother's womb, to the parents who would love, mold and shape me throughout my childhood. Now, as a successful woman of God, I have finally become a person of destiny. I will share the message.

My one and only love; my husband and best friend. I adore you for your sacrifice, encouragement, patience, and support, enabling me to fulfill my dreams and become a complete woman.

My children; J'eannine, Donovan Jr., David and D'anthony. I love you all deeply. Thank you for the sacrifice of love, precious time, and unselfishness, allowing me to complete this project with minimal interruptions.

My wonderful parents; thank you for choosing me. Thank you for the foundation instilled within me. I could not have done it without you. I am now the quintessential daughter, woman, singer and writer because of your love and nurturing. Thank you for your unfailing faith and confidence in my abilities, and for the sacrifice of yourselves, your time and counsel from my beginning to this very important point. I love you.

Miss G and Earl; for life I thank you. I love you for your sacrifice and unselfishness. Thank you for allowing me to share my story. You will always be an important part of my life.

Grandmother, Aunt Marie and Uncle Baz; thank you for the stories, your love and support in this important project. You are the best. I could not have done it without you and I could not ask for more.

Boys; Arthur and Devon, Dave, Wayne and Percival, I am so excited to have you in my life.

To my loved ones, family and friends; you know who you are, I love you. Esther, you are a one in a million sister-friend. To Mom and Dad, Francis, Heather and Chilly, thank you for your love and unselfishness. I am eternally grateful. I would not have made it without you. Samara, my new sister-friend, thank you for taking the time to share your words of inspiration and truth.

To my Editor, Kerri, I could not have completed this project without your valuable input and your keen eye. God Bless you my sister.

Witty Writings, Nathan and company; thank you for becoming an important part of my life and for allowing me this opportunity to share my story with the world.

Mother Smith, thank you so much for your guidance during my beginning days of putting my story together. You were very instrumental to me and I hold you dear in my heart.

To my Pastor, thank you for seeing what God has placed deep within me. For your prayers, instruction, concern and guidance, I will always appreciate you.

To all of you, the audience across the world; may you find healing, peace, and strength as you become the complete men, women, boys and girls you were destined to be. Embrace your journey and live!

Table of Contents

Introduction

Share my journey, beginning in a safe place, tucked inside my mother's womb. After she gave birth, my grandmother and aunt cared for me because my mother was unable. The woman who gave me life was separated from me. As she wrestled with the thought of giving up her first child, a question overshadowed her mind. Was she making the right decision to let her baby go?

For the first six years of life, I was raised in Jamaica. As I transitioned into life with my new parents, I experienced exciting and unforgettable adventures while we ventured to new continents. As I grew into my teenage years, I began wondering why my birth mother had not personally raised me, and I questioned the reasons behind my adoption.

I protected a dark secret in the depths of my soul, of which I shared with no one. My innocence was snatched away without my permission, leaving my confidence in those whom I loved and trusted, broken. I wondered if I would ever experience real love. I was always afraid to ask questions, and knew not who to trust to learn the truth about myself. I yearned to know the truth, my truth, since my family chose not to discuss it with me. My life seemed full of nothing but secrets.

My dreams seemed too far away, as if they were hopelessly unreachable concepts. I found myself on a journey, my journey; a colorful life filled with interesting people, places and experiences, sprinkled with lots of fun and adventure, yet overflowing with unending rivers of emotions. My mind was inundated with mountains of questions, and I was not sure how to find the answers.

I tried my best to mask the empty feelings buried deep within my heart; loneliness and the sense of emptiness that radiated from within the core of my very soul. I became an expert at hiding my disappointments. Communicating my true feelings became a daily challenge. I also developed a fear of forming new relationships, simply because each time I committed to a new one, I found myself alone again. Will my pain ever stop? Can I find true happiness? Can the puzzle pieces of my life fit back together again? Will I ever know the truth? Only time and destiny would tell. Finding the truth revealed God's plan and purpose for my life.

As I embraced the stages of my life, I ultimately found the answers, and healing. My healing was in the clouds. I felt God had forgotten me, but as I learned, the true inner peace I so desperately searched for was unveiled and I found that place of completeness and unquestionable success.

May you enjoy this book, from my heart to yours!

__Please note__: The names of certain persons in this story have been changed or omitted to protect their true identities, at the author's discretion.

About The Author

Evangelist Sharon M. Jones is a Parenting Educator, International Board Certified Lactation Consultant, non-fiction author, dynamic motivational speaker and lecturer, gospel recording artist and International Licensed Evangelist with the Church of God in Christ denomination.

She has worked for over fifteen years with parents and families on the issues of abuse, effective parenting, and family values. Jones attended Rutgers University NCAS and Chabot College. She graduated from Union University in Cincinnati, Ohio with a BA in Maternal Child Health. Jones is currently enrolled in Holy Names University's Master of Arts program and plans to graduate in 2009 with a master's degree in Clinical Psychology and a certification in Pastoral Counseling.

Born in Jamaica, West Indies yet raised in England, the United States, and Africa, Sharon grew up in a Christian home; the daughter of a Pastor-Missionary and a Board Certified Nurse Midwife. She is a third generation musician/singer and a world traveler.

God has given her a divine ability to capture the attention of audiences across the world. With her creativity and calming nature, she continues to create anointed, soul searching, heart transforming, mind regulating melodies; inside the church, the studio, on stage and amongst the many lives she has touched. She has the voice of a messenger. Along with classical piano playing, she adds style and finesse while presenting songs that minister true healing. Sharon creates music and lyrics that are fresh, heartwarming, passionate, and unique; with her gift, she stands out. Her multifaceted ministry, with its dynamic singing and speaking, has touched people worldwide, garnering appreciation and respect.

She is married with four children. Her daughter is in her second year of college. Sharon and her three teenage boys reside in California with her loving husband of 22 years.

Chapter 1

I did not realize the day I sat down to write my story it would signal the beginning of my new journey. At this particular point in my life, I found myself in a place of depression and sadness; somehow, all of my emotions seemed to be on hold. I had to give up the building where I operated my Lactation Consulting business due to low customer clientele and lack of funds. I felt like a failure. I was embarrassed and thought my peers and family would laugh and talk about me because of my failure.

On the Friday evening of the same week I lost my business, I rushed my husband to the hospital as nausea and a cold sweat overtook his body. Once we arrived at the hospital, he was ushered into the emergency room. Within thirty minutes, he was admitted to the intensive care unit with what seemed to be a life threatening diagnosis. My husband remained in the intensive care unit for five days and the doctors took seemingly hundreds of tests, yet they could not pinpoint the root cause of his illness.

I spoke with my mother-in-law later that evening and we decided my brother-in-law would come to California to take two of our children back to Virginia to stay with his family while the other two went to their grandparents home in Florida. This was the first time my children had experienced separation from us, but the arrangement allowed me to focus on nursing my husband back to health. After ruling out a heart attack, the doctors ultimately determined that Rheumatic Fever had attacked my husband's heart. I thank God for healing my husband and restoring his health. Within a couple of weeks, all four of our children returned home and we did our best to resume some sort of normalcy to our lives.

About six months after that life-changing experience, I recall sitting in the living room at my work desk when God began to speak to my heart urging me to write. I remember questioning the Voice of the Lord in a bit of astonishment because I had never actually written a book before. I did not have a clue as to where to begin whatever it was that He wanted me to express on paper. As I remained seated at the desk, I finally decided to obey His voice, picked up a yellow writing tablet, and began scribbling.

For about the first hour, I just scribbled, crumpled up paper and then scribbled repeatedly until I heard the Voice of the Lord speak to me again saying, "Sharon, look deep within your heart and write what I tell you to write." I turned my thoughts internally as I opened up the door to the core of my heart. I remained silent for a brief moment, then I heard the Voice of the Lord say again, "Write about your life, it is within you". The more I scribbled, the more the thoughts began to flow out of my heart and surface into the forefront of my mind. All of a sudden, I found myself writing, "Once upon a time...". I scratched those words and rewrote.

This is where my story begins.

My grandmother said the name chosen for me by my adopted parents if I were born a baby girl was Sharon. I was not told what my name would have been if I was born a baby boy. I made my grand entrance into the world on a late night in June. I was born in 1964 to preacher Farquharson's daughter, on the beautiful Island of Jamaica in the town of Darliston. Darliston is located in the parish of Westmoreland, a place mostly mountainous and heavily wooded. It is spotted with villages of small stucco and wood houses surrounded by fine coral beaches and broad plains where sugar cane, coconuts, and citrus fruits grow in abundance.

Westmoreland expresses a beautiful portrait of rugged coastlines with unforgettably majestic mountains plunging into the borders of the deep blue Caribbean Sea. The capital of Westmoreland is Savanna-la-Mar; a famous seaport town which was known in the early 1940's for processing, refining and exporting sugar cane to various parts of the world.

One unforgettable area in Westmoreland is the magnificent and breathtakingly famous Negril Beach. With its seven miles of pure white sands and indigo blue water, it enchants thousands of tourists year-round from across the world as they sit under coconut trees sipping their tantalizing coconut punch spiked with rum.

The baby blue sky remains peaceful while sprinkled with cotton ball clouds that float day by day. The sugar cane rises grand and tall, trying to touch the sky. The banana trees grow in abundance as their tiny green banana fingers hang neatly tucked together leaning to one side, standing above the rich chocolate brown soil of the earth. The coconut trees rise tall and erect, their branches whispering quietly in the cool summer breeze. The grass runs wild. The ocean waves dance back and forth, as it meets with the coral sand peacefully.

As the pieces of my life began to emerge into the forefront of my mind, I realized in order for me to have a complete story, I needed to obtain some background history on my beginning years. I decided to call my grandmother Sis, my Aunt Marie and Miss G who were all living in New York at the time. This information proved helpful in allowing me to share my journey. With pleasure, these three women opened up my beginning, enabling me to share with you, dear reader.

The unfortunate truth is I only have limited memory of my biological mother being present during the first years of my life. I do not remember seeing her much, or being nurtured by her for a significant amount of time as a small child in Jamaica. We never really developed a meaningful mother-daughter relationship until I turned eighteen years of age. Even now, at times, I recognize our present relationship as more of a biological connection versus a mother-daughter connection. This is a very uncomfortable revelation to express, and at times, I do feel slight regrets.

Allow me to give you a glimpse into my beginning, from the viewpoint and memories of my birth mother, aunt, and grandmother, as told unto me…

Being the daughter of a pastor, Miss G, as I call her in my story, came up in a very strict and extremely sheltered atmosphere by her parents. Her father did his best to direct her every movement in a positive direction, but she was always the unique child. She was free spirited and independent, the one who dared and loved to take on a good challenge.

When Miss G turned nineteen years of age, her father wanted to send her to England to live with her older sibling in order to further her education and become a nurse. However, after much consideration, he changed his mind and decided to send Miss G to a minister friend named Preacher Johnson and his family who lived in Montego Bay, so that she could first obtain a recommendation to further her schooling and become a nurse.

Every weekend starting on Friday evening, Miss G got into a minibus and took the long journey home to Darliston deep in the countryside of the mountains, to spend time with her parents. On Sunday evenings, she returned to Montego Bay to continue her studies. While living at Preacher Johnson's house, Miss G sensed she had an unplanned package. She realized that she might be pregnant. At first, she did not understand the changes taking place inside her body. All Miss G knew was her clothing became uncomfortably tight and she suddenly had an enormously increasing appetite.

The more she ate, the more she desired to eat, and most of her days were spent being nauseous and vomiting at the drop of a hat. Initially, she felt maybe she had eaten some spoiled food, or perhaps she had developed a severe case of food poisoning or perhaps she was catching a serious case of the flu. She could not remember experiencing any other episode like this before.

After several weeks of this continuously uncomfortable feeling, Miss G had no choice but to conclude something was seriously changing deep inside her body. She accepted the fact her condition was not improving but becoming increasingly worse. She had not seen her monthly cycle for four weeks now; of which normally, it would have shown up by this time like clockwork. Her body was feeling significantly different than it had ever felt before.

One Tuesday morning at about six o'clock, Miss G decided to take a mini bus into Savanna-la-Mar town to see Dr. Carnegie, one of the local clinic doctors. To her surprise, after receiving a complete physical, the doctor confirmed that she was definitely pregnant. She was in shock and did not know what to do. The reality of the pregnancy overwhelmed her. She became very nervous, knowing she could not disclose to her parents the disgrace of what had really happened. Not only could she not tell them the truth about what happened, she could not even tell them how or who did it to her. She was hopelessly devastated.

It was still early morning, around nine o'clock, when Miss G left the doctor's office to reluctantly make her way back to Preacher Johnson's house. While reflecting on her plight, the tears seemed to burst up from a spring located deep in the walls of her chest cavity. They flowed down her face and blinded her eyes as she walked on the long dusty road towards home. The sound of the noisy taxies whizzed past her ears, but she was so overwhelmed with her own dilemma, that she did not even take notice of the light brown dust coating her like facial powder. As Miss G suddenly focused back into reality, feelings of despair overwhelmed her, and she realized she was all alone.

She was not sure how to explain this terribly complicated and surprising situation to her father, the preacher. She knew she needed to send him a letter right away, even though she was sure he would never understand. She felt her father would never forgive something like this. She considered the fact he might not even allow her back into his home to live. What she now knew of home would potentially be just mental images of cherished memories. Where were the answers? Who would help in her dilemma? Should she keep this baby or was it better to rid herself of her problem?

For the time being, the best thing was just to wait and intently process her next course of action.

About a month's time passed since the initial doctor's visit. She decided to leave Preacher Johnson and his family to face reality and return home to her parents. Nevertheless, before she left Montego Bay, she decided to share her secret with an elderly woman named Miss Bea, who lived in the neighborhood. The only problem was Miss Bea was the community's town herald and there was no way she would keep her secret. Still, Miss G needed to tell someone, so she decided to take the chance and tell Miss Bea anyway.

As soon as she began to share her secret with Miss Bea about what happened to her, she noticed the twinkle in Miss Bea's eyes because she could not wait for the words to drop from her lips. Miss Bea excitedly said, "Child, tell me everything. I understand. If you do not tell it, I will! So you better just go'n ahead and tell your parents too." Miss G felt a mixed sense of relief and sadness as she regretted ever opening her mouth to share anything with Miss Bea, whom she naively thought could be trusted with her precious secret. The truth of the matter was she ultimately felt a sense of relief as she rid herself of the load she had been carrying on her chest.

After telling Miss Bea about her pregnancy, Miss G decided to stay at Preacher Johnson's for a little while longer; at least until she was about three months into her pregnancy. By then she would have built up the courage to leave and return home to her parents.

The third month had finally passed and the time came for her to return to Darliston. On the morning of her departure, Miss G called for a taxi instead of getting on the overcrowded mini bus for her journey back home into the mountainside. The ride was endlessly long on the winding and bumpy road; it seemed to last about three hours from Preacher Johnson's house in Montego Bay up into the rocky hills of Darliston. As the taxi neared the final corner on the unpaved dirt road leading to the entrance of her parent's gate, Miss G spotted the outline of her mother's petite figure. She was a little distance off, seeming anxious, as she waited to see her daughter again. The taxi came to a screeching stop and the same dusty powder from the dirt road embraced her face again. Her palms were sweaty and her mouth became extremely dry. She opened the door of the taxi while her mother stood at the front gate waiting to greet her. Their eyes immediately connected as she hurriedly exited her seat and closed the door of the taxi.

Her mother glossed her over from head to toe from the gate, and proceeded to run out to the road to meet her. As the warm salty tears collected in the corners of her eyes then flowed gently down her face, with a deep sigh of relief escaping from her lips, her mother uttered slowly under her breath, "Lord have mercy", as she shook her head. Her mother sighed again and wept as she embraced her, allowing the words to escape from her lips, "Lord have mercy, my child has returned home to me." As she turned her around like a graceful ballet dancer turning their partner, she realized her mother noticed something was different about her child, but she just could not figure out what it was. The more her mother twirled Miss G around, the more she realized and confirmed that her daughter was indeed pregnant.

As the two entered the gate to the house, they embraced each other and stood quietly for a moment without saying a word, but just wept together. After what seemed like an eternity, her mother asked in a sympathetically gentle tone "Child, what has happened to you? Let me get a good look at you." Releasing the embrace slightly she said, "I didn't send you away to come back like this. How could you allow this to happen? How is your father going to take this? You know that you cannot stay here! Come, come child quickly, you need food and rest. Let's go inside quietly and we'll figure out what we're going to do later."

Her mother took her by the hand and led her to the back entrance of the house as she shuffled her gently and ever so quietly through the hallway and into her bedroom. Her father heard the commotion and proceeded towards the back of the house only to meet his wife coming out of the back bedroom. He asked, "What's the noise for, Sis? Has Grace come home yet?" Her mother responded, "Yes, but she is tired, she has had a long journey coming from town. Let her rest and you can talk to her later."

Later that evening, after rising from her nap, Miss G shuffled across the immaculately polished hard wood floor of the hallway into the kitchen where her mother was cooking dinner over the open fire. The fire was ever so warm and welcoming and she drew closer to its crackling invitation. Her father was out in the field gathering the farm animals, so it was not time for him to come home yet. Her mother beckoned Miss G to come closer and said to her gently, "Grace, my child, how are you feeling? My heart is crying for you. I do not know what is going to become of you because you cannot stay here. You know that your father won't go for you being in the way."

Miss G dropped her head as the warm salty tears rolled down the sides of her cheeks leaving stain residue on her face. She wiped her face with the corner of her dress, as her mother took her hand, comforting her, and proceeded to ask what happened. Miss G ashamedly lied and told her, "A man, whom I don't even know, befriended me and before I knew what was happening, raped me". She said, "I did not ask to be pregnant, nor did I go looking for trouble, but he just forced himself on me, and before I knew it, the damage had already been done because now, I am pregnant".

After her mother heard the entire story, she told Miss G to be strong and prepare to tell her father the whole truth, no matter what the consequences would be. Miss G realized that days to come were going to be rough for her.

Miss G's parents were very loving but extremely strict, and when it came to rules and discipline, her father remained strong. This meant there would be no unwed pregnant girl living in his house while he preached "hell and damnation" to the rest of the folks.

After about an hour's space of time, she and her mother sat in the kitchen by the old brick fireplace, deeply engrossed in conversation. Simultaneously, they both heard and recognized her father's weary footsteps shuffling through the back yard as he returned home from his day in the field. Miss G's heart palpitated heavily and she felt the pulsation in her throat. She immediately noticed her hands becoming sweaty and clammy. She took a deep breath as she got up and slowly inched her way closer towards her father. He focused in on her movement towards him. He stared into her face, then on her pronounced stomach, and back into her face.

Disappointment overwhelmed him as the rage swelled like an erupting volcano. She saw him hold back the tears as he said angrily, "Girl what is wrong with you! Why do you look the way that you do?" Her mother hurriedly arose from her wooden seat by the old brick fireplace and attempted to serve as a buffer between Miss G and her father. "The child was raped!" she yelled sternly. "She didn't do this willingly", she continued.

"Enough!" was her father's response. "I don't want to discuss this anymore. Our family is an example in the community and I cannot have this. I sent you away to further your education and become a nurse, not for you to meet a man and bring shame to your mother and me. You are a disgrace and you will have to leave this house immediately. You are not welcome here in our home anymore, you must go now!"

Miss G was devastated. She did not know what to do or where to go. She knew no one who would take her into their home for refuge. The sun had already tucked itself away and nightfall had quickly unfolded. No streetlights were there to guide her footsteps. She only had the twinkling stars and the full moon as it reflected with all its brilliance and perfection. No taxies were waiting to escort her to her destination. Not even the sound of an overcrowded mini bus was evident for miles. The melodious songs of hooting owls were heard resonating out of the stillness of the dark night, mixed with the chill of the mountain air.

Miss G felt a sense of fear, and with tear-stained eyes she embraced her mother for the last time. Her mother had packed a little sack with pieces of fried chicken, a few small fried fish, biscuits and a canister of sugar and lemon water for her. It was just enough food to last a couple of days. The last few cents she could scrape together, maybe about two dollars, she gave to Miss G, tied tightly in a handkerchief. Finally, her mother ushered her on her way into the stillness of the dark night. She whispered good-bye, grabbed her sack, and walked out of the house.

Miss G was confused and heart broken. She blew a kiss towards her mother as she stumbled out of the yard onto the rocky and unpaved dirt road. She walked into the darkness without having any sense of direction; there were no streetlights and no paved roads. She did not even have a flashlight to guide her weary footsteps. The sound of the chirping crickets resounded laudably in the atmosphere. Before she realized what was happening, her foot hit a rock, and she felt herself tumbling to the ground. All she could think about was her unborn baby. She could not allow anything to happen to her child. She did her best to fall with her hands stretched out in front of her. Luckily, she was able to catch herself and her bottom hit the ground. Miss G groped around helplessly, frustrated and blinded by the night. As she sat down on the side of the road, the only thing she could do to comfort herself was cry.

After what seemed like an eternity, Miss G struggled back onto her feet, brushed herself off, and continued making her way clumsily through the darkness. Before long, she saw a dim light afar off in the distance. As she came closer, she realized it was the home of her aunt, Miss May. She approached the old squeaky wooden gate, opened it, and stepped up to the front door. She balled her hand into a fist and banged on the door with all the strength she could muster, hoping that someone would hear and take her in from the cold air for the night.

Bang! Bang! Bang! After the fourth bang, she heard a shuffling sound coming towards the wooden door and a fine voice shouted, "Who is it and what do you want?" Miss G responded, "It is me, your niece, Grace." Miss May released the lock and opened the door to let her in. Miss G was shaking and cold from the chill of the night air and was exhausted and famished from the lack of rest and food.

Miss May invited her to come inside and offered her a chair by an old but invitingly warm fireplace. Miss May asked, "What are you doing out on the road by yourself at this hour of the night? How long have you been walking and do you realize that you are two hours from your home?" Miss G responded with a sigh and a long "Yes". With tears collecting in her eyes, she told Miss May she was pregnant, and that she had to leave her parents home because she could not stay there in her condition. After pouring out her heart and soul, Miss May hushed her and told her to rest for a short while from her troubles. However, Miss G would have to leave her house as well because she could not keep her there either. After about four hours of rest, she left Miss May's house and ended up sleeping beneath an oversized mahogany tree under the backdrop of the dark gray sky slightly glittering with the fading of the twinkling stars. She used her food sack to cover a small part of her upper body while her bare arms became her pillow and her warm salty tears were her comfort.

The next morning, she awoke to feel the brightness of the sun embracing her face, as she slowly opened her eyes to meet the clear blue sky. She opened the mouth of the sack, took out a couple pieces of the chicken, one of the small fried fish and biscuit, and began to eat. The food was obviously cold, but tasted ever so delicious.

After satisfying her stomach with food, Miss G stood up from her resting place and started on her way to another woman's house of which she knew named Miss Woods. As she neared the entrance of the yard to Miss Wood's house, Miss G stepped up onto the three wooden, creaking steps and proceeded to the front door. She swallowed her saliva slowly, and raised her fist and knocked gently on the wooden door, hoping someone would hear her from behind the door and come out to rescue her. A woman came to the door, opened it slightly, and asked her what she wanted.

Miss G begged for some warm food and a little hot tea. She lied and told Miss Woods that she was on her way to town for an appointment, and because she had left home so early, she had developed some indigestion in her chest and she just needed to stop for a little while to rest and eat some warm food, and drink a cup of hot tea.

Miss Woods ushered her into the front room of her house and invited her to sit down. After eating some of the warm food and drinking her cup of hot tea, she rested her weary body briefly in one of the back bedrooms. Not long after laying down, she fell into a deep sleep and was able to get some well-deserved rest for just a few hours.

As the community began to come alive with the daily morning routines, Miss G got up from the bed, picked up her sack and slipped out of the house while Miss Woods was in the back of the yard, feeding her goats and chickens. Miss G scurried down the few steps and out the front gate, before Miss Woods could figure out her lie or her pregnancy.

It was another long day and before she realized, it was well into the evening. She had spent the entire day walking alone; not really knowing where she was going and nightfall had embraced her once more. She came to a place of extreme weariness. Exhaustion enveloped her being. She found herself ready to collapse at the gate of another relative's house named Cousin Cook. Cousin Cook took Miss G into her home, and allowed her to stay for a few weeks.

Cousin Cook had seven children and while Miss G stayed at the house, she experienced moments of abuse, mistreatment, and neglect. She became the house cleaner for the family, doing all of the cooking over the hot outdoor wood-burning stove. When she cleaned the house, she buffed the hard wood floors on her knees with a coconut brush and an old piece of cloth.

By this time, she was well into her second trimester, about six months pregnant. It was becoming quite cumbersome for her to move about. She found it challenging to stoop down to clean the floor. Daily, her two swollen hands became the washing machine, as she rhythmically pounded the clothes on the rocks by the side of the riverbank. The hot sun beat vehemently upon her back as the cold water from the river washed across her tired feet and swollen ankles; while the warm salty tears from her eyes rolled down her face. The family entertained themselves as Miss G searched for comfort in her daily chores.

While the family slept nice and snug in their own beds during the night, Miss G snuck around the kitchen like a mouse in search of left over scrapings of food. Every evening, she dragged her weary body to bed. She ached so badly from head to toe; from the pressure of being pregnant and from her daily chores. Her tears and the gentle movement and kicking of her unborn child reminded her that she was not alone, comforting her until she fell asleep.

At the same time Miss G was going through this experience with her relatives, her mother sensed that something was desperately wrong with her child. She had not heard a word from Miss G since the night of her departure. Her mother began inquiring around Darliston, hoping that someone had seen or heard from Miss G. Once the word circulated to enough people, a woman came and told her mother that Miss G was staying at Cousin Cook's house, which was located about two towns away. Upon receiving the news of her child's whereabouts, her mother breathed a great sigh of relief.

At daybreak, Miss G's mother made her way to Cousin Cook's house. While there, she told Miss G that she had something very important to discuss with her. She hesitantly brought up the topic of allowing her sister and brother-in-law, who lived in England, to adopt the baby. Miss G looked at her with a sense of sadness as the tears welled in her eyes and began to flow down her face, like drops escaping from a leaking faucet. Miss G seemed stunned and suddenly disconnected from the conversation with her mother. She secretly felt a slight sense of relief, but she could not express her true feelings in front of her mother.

She was still unable to process the reasoning behind the question presented to her. How could her mother suggest such an idea? Why would she want Miss G to give away her baby after all she was going through? This was not what she wanted to hear or think about at this particular time. Miss G felt a sense of hopelessness as she looked at her mother seeking a better explanation.

Her mother decided to divulge the missing pieces of information. She had already contacted Miss G's sibling and spouse in England. After explaining the situation to them, they were willing to adopt the baby and provide a loving and caring environment in their home. She further said they would provide for the baby in ways that she never could.

Her mother stressed that this was the only chance for the child to experience any kind of fulfilling life.

After thinking about this proposition for a moment, Miss G released another sigh and concluded she would think about the idea and give her mother an answer later. After their discussion, her mother asked how she was managing. Miss G shared how her relatives had misused her and she did not want to stay at their house anymore. Her mother arranged for Miss G to return to Darliston to live with Miss Betts, a country midwife who would ultimately perform her delivery.

Within a few days of the visit from her mother, Miss G returned to Darliston, settled in with the country midwife, and finally decided to reveal the truth behind the identity of her baby's father. Miss G sent word that she wanted to talk to him about the baby he was about to have. The truth of the matter was he came from the same district as Miss G, so her parents knew him and his family very well. His name was Earl and he was twenty years older than Miss G, who at this time was just nineteen years of age.

After sending word to Earl about the impending birth of his child, he sent word back to Miss Betts that he would come and see her within the week. As promised, Earl arrived at the house where Miss G was staying and said he was going to ask her parents if he could marry her. Earl expressed his remorse for getting Miss G pregnant and desired to take responsibility for what he had done by proposing marriage. Her parents expressed their disappointment and told him they would rather he not marry Miss G, but allow her to have the baby and move on with her life by finishing her education.

Earl left immediately and did not visit their house anymore. He decided to stay away from Miss G until after the baby was born. He did not give Miss G any type of financial or emotional support. Therefore, her sister and husband sent monthly assistance and supported Miss G until the day she gave birth.

While Miss G was in the last trimester of the pregnancy, she began experiencing heart problems. After a visit from the clinic doctor, he concluded one of the valves in her heart was not functioning properly. He ordered bed rest for the remainder of the pregnancy so that she would not become overexerted or put the baby in any danger. At eight and a half months, and in spite of her medical condition, she was determined to see the pregnancy through to the very end. She was determined to bring her child into the world.

In the neighborhood, there was an old woman whose name was Nanah. Her profession was to offer abortions to girls who did not want to keep their babies. Nanah heard about Miss G and sent word that she wanted to see her about something important. Nanah did not realize that Miss G was too far into her pregnancy to have an abortion. Miss G left the midwife's house without her consent and went on foot to the place where Nanah lived.

As Miss G approached Nanah's house, after traveling for about an hour, she suddenly felt a cold sensation rush through her body and began to shake from head to toe. Miss G had heard many scary things about this woman, and could not believe she was about to meet the famous Nanah. She walked slowly up to the door. Nanah's yard was full of weeds. The little wood house was dilapidated and painted a morbid and uninviting charcoal gray. On one side of the house were two small, unattended tombstones. Chickens and a couple of goats roamed freely in the yard, nibbling at the weeds, minding their own business.

Miss G swallowed her saliva, followed by a deep breath. With a faint voice she called out, "Nanah", there was no answer. "Nanah", she said a little bit louder. Finally, there was an eerie and slow response. "Who is it and what do you want?" Miss G was ready to u-turn and make a run for it, but she concentrated and gathered her thoughts as she slowly proceeded forward towards the voice behind the door. "Nanah, you called for me and I am here to see you." A dark skinned, thin framed old woman about seventy years old with wrinkled hands, blood shot eyes, and salt and pepper hair tied with a striped scarf on her head came out of the house.

When she saw Miss G, she cracked a brief smile and said, "Child! What is it you want with me?" Miss G cleared her throat and said, "Ma'am, I got word that you wanted to see me." "What do you want from me?" Nanah continued to look at her and said, "Child, I hear you have something that you want me to take from you." Miss G looked at her shockingly and responded, "No ma'am, I don't know what you're talking about." Nanah said, "Child, the thing in your belly, do you want it or not?" Miss G replied, "Yes!" as she hurriedly turned and scurried towards the gate. She left the old woman's yard as if a streak of lightening had touched her. Miss G could not believe this old woman wanted to take her baby. She was mystified. She felt a sense of anger, total shock, and confusion. She was in disbelief that this woman would want to destroy the baby in her womb. Miss G sobbed. She could feel her heart pounding as it raced like a rush hour passenger train, she was breathing so heavily, while trying to catch her breath and she just could not. She walked as quickly as she could for what seemed to be hours until finally, she arrived at the midwife's house.

Back at home, her father became very ill. The doctor concluded he had Leukemia. Miss G learned her father had taken ill and after hearing the devastating news, she became very sad. By this time, Miss G was nearing the last days before giving birth.

Finally, on that late night in June, I decided to make my entrance into the world with the help of the country midwife. The next day, Earl came to the house to see us. Upon entering the room, Earl approached the bed, took one look at me, picked me up, gave me a kiss on the cheek, and gave Miss G one-half a shilling for me. Miss G said because she was angry, she lied and told Earl that I really did not belong to him.

Miss G told him she had gotten pregnant by one of his friends in the district. She wanted to hurt Earl, because he had not supported her throughout the entire pregnancy. She wanted him to feel just a little bit of the rejection, pain and hurt she had suffered. Earl gritted his teeth, put me back into her arms, and said good-bye. The fact is Earl loved Miss G and wanted to marry her, but he could not bring himself to ask her. He marched out of the house and from that day, until I became an adult and searched for him, Earl never laid eyes on me again.

Months after my birth, there was a rumor circulating around the community that Earl had gotten a job as a farm worker and made his way to America. Once he left, it seems he never returned to Jamaica for a visit. Two months after I was born, my grandmother decided it was time for us to return home. She said the day we arrived, my grandfather was not pleased with the decision and expressed his disproval. After much persuasion, Miss G and her father had a long discussion and she asked for his forgiveness for what she had done. She expressed her remorse for bringing pain, disgrace, and shame to the family. With tears in his eyes, he forgave her for letting him down and the two of them embraced and cried tears of joy together. For the first time, in a long time, Miss G felt a sense of completeness. The emptiness she had been carrying around for all those months dissipated into a faded memory. She finally felt as if she was part of the family again.

My grandmother remembers one pleasant fall day, when I was about five months old and taking a nap, Miss G needed to go into Savanna-la-Mar to run an errand, which would take half of the day. She left me at home with my grandparents. After about one hour of sleeping, I could be heard stirring in my small wooden crib, and began crying. My grandfather was in an adjacent room gritting his teeth as he tried to block out the sound of my crying. He hoped somebody else would hear me and come to the rescue. As the sound of my cries grew louder, my grandmother knew that he wished she would come pick me up. By this time, my crying had become uncontrollable. She watched as he waited for a brief moment, but still no one moved to attend to me. After about ten minutes of piercing noise and chaos, she watched as he proceeded to pick me up so that I would be quiet.

As soon as he picked me up, my crying gradually turned into a whimper until I finally hushed. He smiled, looked into my eyes, and softly whispered, "Child, why are you crying? Don't cry now, Dada's got you. Everything is going to be all right." I let out a coo, whimpered a couple more times, closed my eyes, snuggled my head into Dada's warm neck and fell back to sleep as he tucked me close inside his bosom. Dada had not seen Grandmother standing by the door with the widest grin on her face. She remembers thinking that everything indeed would be all right. From that day, I became my grandfather's pride and joy. He looked forward to the times when Miss G had to run errands in town because this was his opportunity to bond with his granddaughter.

I turned two years old in June of 1966, and the following January my Dada again became gravely ill and took a turn for the worse. Grandmother called for the doctor, who said there was no hope for Dada. The Leukemia had taken its toll and the time was drawing near for him to die. Grandmother became very sad. She had to brace herself for the task of arranging for his ultimate death and burial. By midweek, all the family came together to console each other and the following Sunday at about 6 o'clock in the evening, Dada took his last breath and died. This was a very sad time for the family and for and me because my Dada and I had become so fond of each other, and the relationship between Miss G and Dada was at a strong point.

On Monday morning, three of Dada's family members came to the house to prepare his body for burial. I was sitting in the yard with my Aunt Marie when they arrived. Dada appeared cold, as he lay on the bed. I cannot explain it, but my last memory of seeing Grandfather stretched out on the bed looking stiff, is permanent in my mind. I do not remember the process of them preparing him for burial, but I have a vivid memory of his body lying on the bed in front of me. I remember the block of ice placed on top of his body to keep him cool and the pan under the bed to catch the water as it dripped from the body. I do not remember feeling any sense of fear. I actually remember certain parts of my emotions surrounding the death of my grandfather. I do not recall feeling scared.

I quietly snuck up to the entrance of the room. My aunt took my hand and we watched them prepare his body for burial. We made a u-turn and ran out of the house into my grandmother's arms. Why were the men doing this to my Dada? He needed a blanket to keep him warm instead of ice to keep him cold. No one would give me an explanation as to what was going on. As I looked into Aunt Marie and Grandmother's eyes, I saw the tears bubble up then roll down both their cheeks, as if crying in symphony. This made me sad, and I began to cry with them. That is as far as my memory will allow me to remember.

The funeral was set for Wednesday evening at three o'clock sharp. As the day finally arrived, people came from everywhere to attend the service for my Dada. Grandfather Farquharson was the District Pastor for about four churches and all the church members and people in the community showed up for his home going, in all about 200 people.

I could not understand why they were so happy; there was so much singing and rejoicing. They should have been sad and mournful like my family. Instead of being sad, they seemed glad. They brought ground provision, meat, rice, sweet potato, corn pudding, jelly coconut and sugar cane. These people were happy as if having a great celebration. This was the largest party I had ever been to in my short life. The people were dancing as they beat on tambourines and played guitars, banjos and accordions, while marching around the freshly dug gravesite. My grandmother had Dada Farquharson buried in the churchyard with many of the other deceased pastors and church members.

My new parents were not able to attend the funeral. Within days they sent Grandmother money to buy food, clothing and other necessities until it was time for me to leave Jamaica.

Chapter 2

*A*fter Dada's death, Miss G moved on with her life and went back to Montego Bay to finish her education. Grandmother and Aunt Marie raised me until it was time to leave the Island and live with my new parents in Europe.

I only have a vague memory of my birth mother being in my life during those first few years. The fact of the matter is Miss G was not active in my life during that time. As for Earl, he did not have the privilege of sharing in all the exciting phases in my life.

One not so pleasant memory occurred during the time I was in preschool. I was four and a half years old and I was the smallest in stature within my group of friends and schoolmates. Every morning and evening, while traveling to and from school, we passed an old broken down cemetery by the side of the road. As soon as we neared the graveyard, the kids would run off teasing me. They left me behind; laughing and yelling scary words saying "Duppy", or the ghost, was going to get me.

This scared the life out of me. It left me shaken and afraid. The only thing I knew to do was cry and run for my very life. My books would always end up tossed into a field somewhere near the graveyard. I went through this ordeal every single day. I began having nightmares, waking up in the middle of the night crying out the ghosts were chasing me, begging someone to "wait for me". I also experienced bladder incontinence and would wet myself during sleep.

Aunt Marie would hear my screaming then run into my room, hold me in her arms and rock me back to sleep. Every night, the ordeal seemed to play itself out in my mind. This ended up being a continuously frightening experience for me.

I had a special name for my Aunt; I called her Auntie Mayan.
You see I really could not pronounce her name correctly so she was
"Maya" to me. I had never seen such a beautiful woman as my
Auntie Marie. Her beauty radiated like the sun breaking through on
a warm summer day. She stood about 5ft. 5in. tall, with a light
brown complexion. She had long black hair and brown eyes. She
was petite, only about 130 pounds, and radiated natural beauty and
charm.

Auntie Marie was not married at the time, and she lived with
us until I made my departure for Europe. Auntie Marie was the only
mother figure I knew, along with other children in the community.
She was very kind and patient; always nurturing, and loved me
unconditionally as a mother loves her child. Aunt Marie raised me
as if I was her own biological child. Now keep in mind, not only
was she unmarried at the time, but she was twelve years older than I.
I never wanted to leave her sight and tried my best to do everything
she did, to the best of my little ability.

Each day we went to fetch water from the community water
tank. Since I was so small, Aunt Marie gave me a small bottle to
carry my water while she carried the heavier container full of water.
As I grew and gained strength in my arms, I graduated from the
small water bottle to the small water container. I felt so proud of
myself being able to carry my water as she did each day.

Sunday mornings were a treat because my aunt would dress
me in one of the outfits sent from my parents in England. One of my
favorites was a white ruffled princess dress with pink, yellow and
green embroidered flowers across the front of the bodice and a big
white bow tied neatly in the back. The hair bows and socks always
matched the color of the dress and a pair of black patent leather
shoes and matching handbag complemented the outfit.

Auntie Marie took me to the church before any of the other
children in order to receive the prize for being the first person to
arrive for Sunday school. She taught me all of the favorite songs and
I became a scholar at memorizing Bible verses. Aunt Marie and
Grandmother raised me under their love and protection until it was

time for me to leave the Island. By my sixth birthday, my new parents sent for me.

I remember the day of my departure from Jamaica, in the fall of 1970. I was dressed in a beautiful white dress with a matching white hat, white patent leather shoes, and white bag. This day was full of sadness and tears for everyone, especially Aunt Marie, because the bond between us was so strong and I identified with her as my mother. The bond we shared was about to be broken and I was terrified. I was leaving my place of safety and security, my chickens and my mud pies. I did not want to go.

I dreaded going to this new place called England to live with people who would now be my new mom and dad. I did not want to go to a strange place where I heard the people spoke differently from me. I did not want to leave the place where fields were wide open and covered with green grass, where the white sand and the deep blue sea met as one, where children played without fear of danger in their pure innocence.

The day had finally come for me to leave Jamaica and I bawled, because I did not want to go. As Grandmother, Aunt Marie, some of our close neighbors and I arrived at the Montego Bay Airport, Aunt Marie took my little hand and walked to a remote area in the terminal. With tears filling her eyes and staining her beautiful caramel colored face, she told me to be a good little girl and that she loved me and I had to be brave. She said she was going to miss me but promised to come and visit one day. She gave me the tightest squeeze and kissed me on my cheek as we walked back to the waiting area.

When the time finally came for me to board the airplane, Aunt Marie handed me over to the flight attendant, went back to that remote spot in the terminal, and wept bitterly. I could hear her as she shed tears of sadness for me. I said goodbye to Grandmother as the flight attendant took me by the hand and led me away. To me, these people were strangers. I recall walking down the long runway, out of the airport to the steps of the plane and seeing this gigantic thing that looked like an enormous silver bird. Its wings were so long and ever so wide. It scared me. It stood out as a great big metal giant, like the story in the Bible of little David looking up into the face and terror of the giant Goliath. The airplane seemed very cold and motionless; so uncaring, unloving, and unfriendly. It seemed as if it would gobble me up and never let me go.

As I approached the steps of this huge metal bird, my heart pounded like the sound of a bass drum. The beats kept getting faster and faster, louder and louder, heavier and heavier. It seemed as if my heart moved from my chest cavity up into my throat and was just one step from leaping into my mouth. My steps felt weaker and weaker, heavier and heavier. I felt as if I was walking in wet cement. Each step I took seemed to be even harder with my every move. Oh! If only I could blink my eyes and make this day go away. I hoped this was all a dream. I wished so badly that I could just wake up from this nightmare and everything would be as it was before.

I missed Aunt Marie and Grandmother and wanted to go back home to be with them in Darliston. As the tears welled up I did my best to fight them back. I was trying to be strong like my aunt had asked. The harder I fought back the tears, the more they forced themselves out and rolled down my face onto my white dress. I looked up into the sky. It was such a beautiful day. The sky was bright blue and appeared ever so peaceful. The snow-white cotton ball clouds just rolled by as if saying to me, "Why are you afraid? This is the beginning of the rest of your life! We will always be with you to lead you and guide you". As I reached the last step before stepping into the plane, I looked up to the sky again, amidst my tears and said out, loud, "Laud, mi dead now!" I felt that my world was slowly but surely ending.

The tears in my eyes were blinding me and felt like a rainstorm heavy enough to flood a village. I do not know why I said those words, but it seemed appropriate at the time. The people and things that were dear to me seemed to be leaving. They were getting dimmer and dimmer, and farther and farther away from me. The tears kept rolling down my cheeks gathering at the middle of my chin, making a statement on my white dress. All I could do was wipe the tears away from my eyes with the back of my hand. The more I licked the salty tears away from my cheek, the more they kept coming.

I was all alone. I looked around hoping the people I knew and loved were traveling with me. As I searched all around with my eyes, no one I knew was following behind me. Why was Aunt Marie not coming? Why was Grandmother not coming with me? What was wrong with this picture? I needed answers, but no one would provide the answers I needed.

As I entered the airplane, I remember struggling with the flight attendant. You see I did not want to go on this plane ride, so I stubbornly refused to sit down and put on my seat belt. After much coaxing, I reluctantly proceeded to my seat and sat down by myself. Tearfully and reluctantly I prepared to take my journey.

The flight attendants tried their best to make me feel better by offering me food, drink and sometimes a snack. They even tried to play games with me, all to no avail. I was not interested in anything or anyone at that moment. All I wanted to do was turn around, get off the airplane, and go back to my family. The plane ride was very long and I spent most of the flight sleeping.

After, what seemed like a lifetime in the sky, the airplane landed in a strange place called London. The first sights I saw while exiting the plane were very beautiful, things I had never seen before. I viewed the tall buildings and a great big river. The airport seemed three times as large as the one in Montego Bay. The people did not look like me. They were lighter than me and I was not quite sure why they looked so different.

The flight attendant and I walked through the terminal hand in hand then she turned me over to a man and woman I had never seen before. They were my new parents whom Aunt Marie had told me so much about. As they greeted me, I was in awe with the beauty of their accent. It was like the words just rolled off their tongues. They seemed so warm and inviting. They embraced me with many affectionate kisses and lots of love. I felt as if something deep inside my stomach settled.

Before I realized it, all of my fears and apprehensions seemed to vanish and the biggest smile came across my face. For one moment, I remembered those snow-white cotton ball clouds that greeted me when I boarded the plane in Jamaica. I knew that somehow everything would be all right.

Chapter 3

*W*hile in England, I lived in a country town called Crewe. This is where the "Railway Works", which is famous for its steam locomotives, is located. Crewe is a small but beautiful town, with green open spaces and an unforgettable picture of nature. My parents made sure I had a privileged and happy childhood. I had the best of everything a 6-year-old child could ever need or want.

I attended the best private schools, where I wore navy blue uniforms with white starch-pressed blouses. Every day I went to school, my uniform was always pressed and pleated ever so neatly. I was always matching from head to toe. While attending school, I had the privilege of having swimming lessons on Friday afternoons for one hour at a time. Within a short period, I knew how to swim very well.

The house we lived in was called a flat, or a townhouse. Behind these flats were green open fields where the cows grazed undisturbed and carefree by the railroad tracks, which ran beside a cool flowing brook. Many days after school, I would play and run with my father in the open fields. It was so peaceful and serene.

One day, I looked up into the sky and noticed what seemed to be those same snow-white cotton ball clouds that I had seen the day I left Jamaica. Again, the clouds were saying to me, "We told you this was the beginning of your life, and we will always be with you." At that moment, I smiled and seemed to agree.

Chapter 4

*W*hen I was about seven years old, I met a girl by the name of Cindy who lived in the adjacent flat with her grandmother. Cindy was about seven years older than me and I loved spending time with her. The two of us shared stories and fun times together. We loved sharing jokes with one another.

One particular joke Cindy shared with me was about a woman who had a bad eye. As Cindy told the joke, she would turn her eyelids inside out pretending to be the woman in the story. Each time Cindy did this I became scared out of my wits. After hearing the bad eye story several times, my imagination ran wild and I began to have nightmares.

Every night as I fell asleep, I imagined the woman with her eyelids turned inside out chasing me. I screamed at the top of my lungs, "Wait for me, wait for me! Please don't get me, and don't leave me!" My father would come into my room and wake me. I was shaking like a leaf as beads of cold sweat stretched across my forehead.

I continued wetting my bed and this was an uncomfortable problem for me. My father would stay with me, or if she was off from work that particular night, my mother would stay with me until I drifted back to sleep. In the early hours of the morning, my father left me sleeping in bed while he went to pick up Mother because she worked the night shift at the hospital.

One day, during the early hours of the morning, while Father left to pick up Mother from the hospital, I awoke out of my sleep. I began screaming at the top of my lungs, because I had another nightmare about the woman with the turned over eyelids. I dreamt she had been chasing me. I got up out my bed, with tears in my eyes yelling, "Wait for me, wait for me! Please do not leave me!" I ran out the front door of the flat and down to the gated compound, barefoot in my wet nightgown. Within a matter of minutes, Father's car pulled into the complex and he spotted me running in the yard. He stopped the car, told Mother to park and began running after me. Once he reached me, he grabbed my hand, lifted me and held me close in his arms as he carried me back into the flat. I was shaking like a frightened pup. I was terrified and crying. Father held me close as he asked what happened. I told him about my dream. Father shook his head, smiled and held me close as he carried me back to my room and into bed. He stayed with me until I fell asleep.

Father called my aunt in Jamaica to investigate the cause behind my bad dream episodes. Aunt Marie informed him that while passing a cemetery walking to and from school the children made fun of me; saying the ghosts were going to get me, and then they would run off and leave me. Father was now able to understand exactly what was going on in my mind. He decided to have a talk with me and explained that what those children did was wrong, and he would never allow any thing bad to hurt me in any way as long as he lived. The bad dreams continued to haunt me for a few months and my parents were always there to console me until I built up enough courage to finally gain control over my fears and the bad dreams. With time, and much love, I began feeling better, and from that day on, I gradually experienced less traumatic dreams.

It was customary for Father to walk me a part of the way to school in the mornings as Mother's work schedule would not allow her to do so. He was the one that combed my hair, prepared breakfast, and helped start my day. Father pushed his bicycle next to me as we walked to the place where we parted ways for the day. As we came to that spot in the road, Father gave me a kiss on the cheek and bid me good day. We then parted our ways until later that evening.

One particular day after Father and I had parted ways, I came across a Caucasian boy who loved to wait for me behind the bushes. He made it a point of duty to jump out of the bushes and taunt me. This annoying boy's name was Peter and he was about 7 years old, the same as I. Peter enjoyed teasing and taunting me. He would call me names like "little dark girl" and "brownie" for no apparent reason.

The verbal abuse irritated me so intensively that I made up my mind to do something about the situation. That evening, while Mother and I were washing the dinner dishes, I began talking about the activities of my day. I told her about Peter and how he constantly taunted me on my way to school.

Mother asked me to describe exactly what Peter did and I explained that he called me names like the "N" word and "Blackie" and made fun of me. I expressed how he humiliated me and caused me to feel a sense of fear. Mother thought for a minute and then offered some advice on how to take care of Peter for the last time. She told me if I followed her advice, she could almost guarantee he would not bother me again. She told me I had to learn how to stand up to Peter and beat him at his own game. She said the next time he taunted me I should look into his eyes, put my foot out and trip him, then he would leave me alone.

The next morning as Father and I parted our ways, Peter again jumped out of the bushes and started his taunting. I thought for a quick second about what Mother suggested and decided to take her advice and act as if I was not afraid of Peter. I kept my attention focused on where I was going, but then I decided to stop and deal with him.

I turned my gaze towards him and stretched my foot out. As he proceeded toward me, he did not see my foot and started to fall as I ran away. I turned around to see why he stopped. I realized while he was caught up with his taunting and playfulness, "Poof", he went down, hitting his nose as he made contact with the ground. I was so terrified, but inwardly I was laughing.

Before I knew it, Peter was focused on the embarrassment and humiliation of having fallen to the ground. I held my breath for a brief second, and looked to see if he was all right. After reassuring myself that he was going to be ok, I walked over and extended my hand to help him back on his feet. Laughing outwardly at him, I helped him up, and said, "Next time, you will not taunt me or make fun of me, because it appears that what you dished out is what you just got". Peter looked at me. Disgusted with himself, he offered a half corner smile, and responded, "Yeah, I guess you are right."

From that day, Peter never taunted me or called me any offensive names. I decided I would not allow him to get the upper hand of me. I felt empowered and knew I could handle any other person that came to harass or ridicule me. After he collected himself and his books, Peter and I proceeded to make our way to school. After that episode, Peter and I became the best of friends. Instead of having an enemy, I had a friend to walk me to school everyday.

My mother was a nurse-midwife at the hospital and one of the most enjoyable activities for me was to go with her to look at the babies in the nursery. Mother had delivered at least 500 babies, and it was quite regularly a treat for me to visit with her on a weekly basis. My father worked in the factory as a carmaker. He assembled cars at the Rolls Royce plant.

On Saturday mornings, from 9:00 to 10:00am I had piano recitals. My teacher Mrs. Hopkins was a renowned pianist. She was an old woman who was very kind yet firm when it came to her students. She held the music lessons in the front parlor of her home. I always enjoyed going over to Mrs. Hopkins home. At the end of each lesson, we would share tea and biscuits. This was our special weekly routine. She took time out for me and always showed gentleness and patience. She made sure I was well prepared, for both my exams and recitals. Mrs. Hopkins helped to build confidence in myself as a student and a human being. She empowered me to believe in my piano playing abilities. I always came away from her recitals winning either first or second place in the various competitions. I had a special love for Mrs. Hopkins, and she displayed the same love for me.

Fridays were my favorite. Every Friday when Father received his paycheck he took Mother and I out for dinner. It consisted of either Chinese food or fish and chips, distributing its pungent vinegar aroma through the newspaper onto your hands and any other surface it met. I loved to smell the rich scent of the fish and the newspaper mingling together as one. I could not wait for Friday evening to come along, because it meant I was going to enjoy one of my favorite meals.

One place I did not enjoy visiting was the dentist. When I moved to England from Jamaica, I had a mouth full of rotten teeth, so the first thing my parents did was arrange for me to visit the dentist quite often in order to receive proper oral care. I was told the reason for my deficiency was due to Miss G not consuming enough calcium while pregnant, so I was born having very weak teeth. Unfortunately, I was a bleeder, and with every procedure I was put to sleep before any extractions on my teeth. I did not particularly enjoy this, but it was an experience that will always be a significant part of my history.

Not only did my father work at the car plant, but he was also the pastor for one of the local churches. A few Sunday mornings during services, as the offering was being collected, I felt the urge to become a little bit mischievous. I got up from my seat as the other parishioners, as saintly as I could, and proceeded towards the front of the church where the offering buckets were placed. I reached my hand into the bucket, pretending to put a coin in. Instead, I scooped up a couple of coins, and kept on walking back to my seat with the money neatly tucked into my hot palm. I chuckled to myself as I sat down to enjoy the rest of the service. I knew I would be ready to supply my friends with their Monday morning candy for the entire week.

I kept this up for a few more Sundays until I finally paid attention to the conviction screaming loudly from my heart, telling me that what I was doing was wrong. I decided to give up stealing. Father never suspected or found out. I was relieved that he and Mother did not have a clue to the evil thing I had done.

Chapter 5

Summers were the fondest season of the year for my family because we always went away for a summer holiday. One particular summer, when I was the age of nine, my family was invited by one of Mother's colleagues, Dr. Mann, to visit his family's summer home in Scotland for three weeks. I was so excited about the invitation and looked forward to the trip with anticipation.

On the day of our departure, we took the train to Scotland. I enjoyed viewing miles and miles of open meadows, rich rolling farmlands and rugged seacoasts. On one side of the train, I saw hazy blue hills running out to the wide horizon, and the experience lifted my heart and spirit. On the other side of the train, I viewed the mountain scenery and the dramatic coastline. The air was fresh with the smell of summer. The cows could be seen grazing in open meadows, right next to the brook gently flowing down the countryside. The white sands met the deep blue sea. The snow-white cotton ball clouds rolled above the train and I heard in my subconscious, "We are still here with you and always will be as long as you live".

When we arrived in Scotland, I looked around and saw people staring at us as if we were aliens from Mars. I looked up at Mother and Father, and then I looked down at the backside of my hands. I wondered what was so intriguing about us to these people. Why were they staring so intently?

As we disembarked from the train and started mingling in the crowd, I wondered to myself why the people were staring. I thought maybe my face looked disfigured, or maybe I had messy food stains on my clothing. I felt uncomfortably awkward and out of place.

The more I paid attention to people's eyes; I started figuring out what was so peculiar to them. As I saw more and more people looking at us strangely, my intuition became clear as I noticed one thing. No other black people were around. You see, the people were not accustomed to seeing blacks around them; and it was probably strange to see us dressed so well descending from a personal coach in the train.

After waiting at the train station for about five minutes, Dr. Mann and his driver came up to the station and beckoned with a wave of the hand to us. We embraced and then were ushered into the black limousine with smiles, hugs, kisses and a lovely bouquet of flowers. The journey to Dr. Mann's home lasted only about 20 minutes as we took the scenic route.

The breathtakingly blue ocean swayed peacefully next to the road as the seagulls echoed their songs to each other while flying high above the tiny rippling waves. Finally, we neared the majestic looking blue Victorian house. The car turned into the tall black iron gates and then proceeded down the long winding driveway. I opened my mouth and gasped in awe at the beauty and splendor of what I saw; a two-story house that was so picturesque.

It was impressively manicured with colorful flowers of every description and splendor, which struck a chord with my senses. It looked like a fairytale house out of the pages of a storybook. Across the street from the house was the deep blue ocean.

The seagulls were still flying in the air, talking to each other. The ocean seemed to be saying "Hush, hush, shh, hush, hush, shh". The sky was ever so blue and those snow-white cotton ball clouds were just rolling by. I smiled and waved to the clouds as we rode to the side lawn of the house and the car came to a stop. As the driver opened the door, I heard dogs barking. Suddenly I noticed there were two enormous but beautiful black dogs coming to meet their master and his guests. I swallowed. You see, I had never experienced such things and was not ready to be the main course meal for these beasts, nor did I desire to receive a slobbering welcome.

I hesitated to emerge from the car behind my parents. Dr. Mann noticed my fear and stretched out his hand to bid me come. He told me the dogs were friendly and would do no harm, so I need not be afraid. After thinking about it for a moment, I decided to proceed from the car. I took the doctor's hand and made sure to squeeze it ever so tightly, just to let him know that I was scared and needed his protection.

Before I knew what was happening, the two black dogs jumped up on me and started licking my face. I screamed and froze in my tracks, deciding not to move another step with these ferocious beasts jumping all over me. Dr. Mann firmly said "Emily, Spot, No! Down!" The dogs backed off and went their way as if they had been insulted. We quickly went into the house and I released a sigh of relief.

As we entered into the kitchen, there was a short and pleasant looking woman in a flowery printed dress with a white apron tied around her waist waiting by the table. She came over and hugged me tightly. Dr. Mann introduced her as his wife Margaret. A burst of laughter resounded off the walls of the kitchen. From there we all ventured into the sitting room and started to converse. In the corner was positioned a caramel-colored rocking horse, with large black eyes. Its eyes were so fixated and focused that they appeared to be looking directly at me. It seemed to be saying, "Would you like to ride me?" I looked intently back at the horse and thought in my mind, "I am going to ride you when I get ready". It seemed as if Mrs. Mann was in on the conversation between us. She asked if I wanted to ride the horse. I attentively said, "Yes please".

As I began riding the horse, someone closed a door from the kitchen. I looked up and saw a young man entering the sitting room. He was tall, dark and handsome, with jet-black hair and the bluest eyes I had ever seen. My heart went pitter-patter and seemed to skip a beat. I was infatuated with this young man at the tender age of nine. I began to blush and dropped my head. The young man was introduced to us as Doug. He was only child of Dr. and Mrs. Mann. I think he was about 24 years old. For the rest of the evening, I did my best to wander around the house looking for Doug. Every room that Doug entered, I followed right behind, until he left the house and did not return until late that night. I did not know if he had a girl friend or not, but I really did not care. I was just happy to have him in the house.

The next morning after breakfast, Doug gave me a big hug, and asked if I wanted to go for a walk on the beach with him and the dogs. I thought I was going to pass out. I could not believe I was being invited by this handsome creature to go for a walk. I was beside myself with joy. The beach was across the street from the house. Without hesitation, I said yes.

We left with the dogs and proceeded to walk across the street to the beach. By this time, the dogs and I had overcome our fear of each other and were now great friends. The ocean water was warm as it bathed our bare feet. It was a deep blue color, and the antique white sand met the ocean just at the edge and the two came together as one. One could see and hear the seagulls as they made their crash landings into the water looking for food. The air was so warm and delightful. Quite a number of people were on the beach, just enjoying the beauty of the day. As I focused on the people around me, I realized there were a few with features just like me. I released a big sigh of relief and felt a bit more at ease with my surroundings. Each morning from that day until we left Scotland, Doug, the dogs and I ran alongside the beach playing and laughing as if we had not a care in the world.

Scotland was one of the most breathtaking, magnificently beautiful places on God's green earth. The three weeks flew by quickly and after an unforgettable vacation, the day finally came for us to return to England. I was very sad. The morning of our departure, I reluctantly got dressed. All of us, Dr. and Mrs. Mann, Doug, my parents and I, ate breakfast together and then it was time for us to leave. Outside, I heard the smooth engine of that same black car pull into the driveway to take us back to the train station. Everybody said their good-byes, and then it was time for us to go.

Once we arrived at the terminal and boarded the train, we located our private coach and settled in for the journey. As we got comfortable in our seats, Father noticed the tears rolling down my cheeks. He placed his arms around me and asked what was wrong. I told him I had a bad toothache and that my head was hurting me. Father knew better but he just hugged me and said nothing while he smiled at Mother and we made our way home.

Chapter 6

*B*efore age ten, I met a girl who was about two years older than I named Lillieth. Lillieth and I developed a deep sister friendship. We were mischievous together, always played together, and did all the things that little girls do; like playing with dolls, hop scotch and playing school.

We shared many conversations about our dreams and about the future. We talked about what we wanted to be when we grew up. We were planning to be pediatric doctors and live in the same town, next door to each other. We would have identical cars and the same color houses. We even planned to marry on the same day and have two children just the same. We both wanted a girl and a boy. We were inseparable.

Lillieth was sick quite often. You see she had Sickle Cell Anemia, an inherited blood disease that occurs primarily in people of African decent. Lillieth would get tired very easily and always had headaches. We could never run long distances, because Lillieth would always be out of breath. Every time she caught a cold, she became very sick.

One particular day, while on summer break from school, on a clear Wednesday afternoon, Lillieth and I were playing house in her back yard and she suddenly started to cry. I felt a sense of fear envelope my being as I looked at Lillieth directly in her eyes and asked what was wrong. Lillieth tried to tell me she had a terrible stomachache and was feeling pain from the crown of her head to the soles of her feet.

I stopped what I was doing, ran inside the house, and called Lillieth's mother. We both went back out to the yard where we found Lillieth vomiting as the diarrhea crawled down her legs. Before I realized what was happening, my best friend Lillieth had collapsed and fallen to the ground. Her mother ran inside and called for Lillieth's father who came out side and picked up her frail and limp body. He put her into the back seat of their car with her mother at her side, while yelling back at me to hurry home to tell my mother what had happened. They sped off to the hospital and I stood in the backyard motionless; feeling a sense of helplessness, not knowing what to do. As I remember this precious memory, feelings of sadness resurface and tears embrace my eyes.

I regained my sense of focus and ran back home without thinking to tell Mother what happened. I cried uncontrollably as I fell into Mother's arms. My words and crying crossed and seemed to come out of my mouth at the same time as mumble jumble and Mother just held me as she tried to calm me down. "What's wrong Sharon? What's wrong with you?" I proceeded to rehash what happened to Lillieth and how her father had told me to hurry home to share the bad news. I could see the concern on her face and she did her best to calm me down. Mother encouraged me to go into her room and lie down. Shortly thereafter, I consoled myself and drifted off to sleep.

When Lillieth's parents arrived at the hospital, they parked the car at the emergency entrance where her doctor anxiously awaited their arrival. He then rushed her into the emergency room. The doctor quickly examined Lillieth and asked what happened before they arrived. Her mother proceeded to explain that Lillieth had been playing outside when all of a sudden she started crying and complaining of severe stomach cramps and diarrhea. After getting a complete history from her parents, the doctor immediately ordered a variety of tests to determine what exactly was happening to Lillieth. The nursing staff gently and sympathetically ushered her parents into the family waiting area until they were finished examining her.

About an hour later, the doctor returned to the waiting room looking rather grim. He walked towards Lillieth's parents and informed them she was dying and the only thing that could be done was to take her back home. He told them the disease had taken its toll on her small body and Lillieth would die shortly. Lillieth's parents proceeded slowly into the examination room to dress their child and take her home to die peacefully. With tears in his eyes, Lillieth's father picked her up and placed her frail and barely responsive body into the back seat of the car.

Her mother rested Lillieth's head gently on her lap as they started their long and mournful journey home. At the same time, back at my house, I awoke from my nap and Mother and I impatiently awaited the news of Lillieth's condition. I looked at the clock on the wall in Mother's room and it said eight o'clock in the evening.

While Lillieth's parents were driving home, the car reached a speed of 80 miles per hour; there was a loud bang and an exploding noise, which caused the car to come to sudden dramatic stop. Lillieth's mother was abruptly repositioned to the other side of the back seat as the car swerved to the opposite side of the road. The car came to a dead stop. Lillieth's father exited to see what had taken place. Upon raising the front end, he realized the radiator had blown. He panicked because he needed to get her home. After about 30 minutes of waiting for a Good Samaritan to come by, a brown 4-door car with a young couple approached them. They stopped next to Lillieth's father and offered their assistance.

Lillieth's parents had to abandon their vehicle because it was inoperable. Her father lifted her out gently as the young stranger opened the back door of his car. Lillieth's mother sat motionless. Her father touched his wife on the hand as he calmly encouraged her to come out and get into the back seat of the other vehicle. He then positioned Lillieth with her head resting in her mother's lap. Lillieth's father entered the couple's car on the opposite side of the back seat and they all proceeded to make the journey home to Crewe. Sadly, on the way, Lillieth took her last deep breath and expired. Her father looked at his watch. It was 9:45 in the evening.

Lillieth's parents were distraught and with all the strength her father could muster, he asked the couple if they would take Lillieth's body back to his home where he could call the family doctor. When the doctor arrived, he examined Lillieth, and pronounced her officially dead. The time was 10:45pm.

It was a sad time for Lillieth's parents and the community. After the doctor left, her father called my parents to inform them of her passing. My parents did not want to wake me. They decided to wait until the next day to share the devastating news.

Thursday morning came as another usual day; however, the sky was gray and the clouds hung low as I got out of bed and dressed for another day to spend with Lillieth. I decided that because I had not heard anything from her yet, she must have still been asleep. I was going to make my usual trip over to her house not to play with her, but just to visit. I was not sure if she had made it back from the hospital, but I wanted to check just in case she had returned home.

As I was dressing, Mother came into my room. When I looked into her eyes, I felt something was wrong, but I did not know what it was. She beckoned me to come and sit down beside her on the bed. Mother gave me a big hug, and told me that she loved me. She looked into my eyes and said she had some sad news. She told me something bad had happened to Lillieth.

She said Lillieth had gone away from earth to live with Jesus and I would not be able to go and play with her anymore. I looked at Mother as I felt my world crumbling and asked her what she meant. Mother said Lillieth had gone into a deep sleep, one she would never wake out of again. I cried.

I was confused, I felt hopeless. Why would Lillieth do such a thing like this to me? We had not completed all of our planned dreams yet. We had not planned our weddings, we had not had our children. How dare she do this to me? She was not supposed to leave me like this; we were supposed to be inseparable forever. Lillieth did not even say good-bye to me. This was not how the story was supposed to end. What would happen to our plans for the future? We had dreams that had not come true yet. I could not go on without Lillieth. In that moment of sadness, I wanted to go home to live with Jesus too. I wanted to be where Lillieth was. Those same tears that visited me the day I left Jamaica, came back into my eyes, and bubbled up so that I could hardly see. Tears rolled down my cheeks evenly on both sides. They came together in the center of my chin and dripped onto my outfit, making another statement. I was oh so sad.

I felt like someone had reached deep into my chest, through my rib cage, yanked my heart out, then tossed it to the ground and stomped it to death. I wanted to die. I did not see any reason for living anymore. How could I go on without my precious Lillieth? Whom would I talk to? Who would understand me? Who would share my dreams and my plans for the future? I was devastated. I became speechless. Mother told me to finish dressing quickly so we could comfort Lillieth's mother. I cried and cried. My tears would not stop coming. It seemed as if the very ocean I had walked beside in Scotland was rising inside of me and I would never stop crying for the rest of my life.

Lillieth's funeral was on Saturday; a cold, foggy, unfriendly day. I woke that morning without having much to say. I proceeded to get dressed. Mother had bought the most beautiful white long sleeved cotton dress with a large bow centered in the small of my back. I went into the sitting room to wait for the hired car to come and take us to the funeral. My heart felt very heavy and empty. As we proceeded to the church, I began to cry.

As we neared the church, we saw the parking lot full with cars. When we entered the chapel, there were what seemed to be hundreds of people. I entered the front door and walked bravely down the center isle by myself. As I approached Lillieth's casket, I admired what I saw. The casket was a beautiful snow-white color. It was smaller than a regular casket. Lillieth lay there quietly as if she was taking a nap.

She was dressed in a beautiful white lace dress that reached below her knees. She had white gloves on her hands, long white socks and white shoes on her feet. They placed a white Bible in her hands. She looked so peaceful. She had the most beautiful smile on her face. She seemed to be saying, "Sharon, my friend, my sister, why are you crying, do you see me crying? I am fine. Everything will be all right". Lillieth appeared as if she was simply asleep.

I wanted so badly to say to Lillieth, "Quit kidding and open your eyes". Since we were so close and played so many silly games, maybe this was one of them. Lillieth was only 12 years old. I stood by the casket for a few moments hoping and praying that my friend would get up, but she never did. In addition, we never got the chance to say good-bye! I was scared and went to my seat beside Mother. After the one-hour service, my parents and I went to the gravesite for the internment. I started thinking I was going to die just like Lillieth when I turned 12. I was only nine.

Chapter 7

*A*s I turned 10 years of age, Father applied to Northwest Bible College in America and was approved for admissions to the school. He had a desire to further his studies as a minister.

In the spring, when Father received his final confirmation letter from the Bible College, he shared the exciting news that we were moving to America. Father was going to get the opportunity to finish his education and better himself as a pastor. He would leave Mother and I for a brief period of time, approximately three months duration, then Mother and I would be rejoining him in America.

I became very sad. My parents and I had never been away from each other for such a long period and this was going to be a first-time experience for me. I felt like I did on the day when I got the news that Lillieth had passed away. Those same tears came back, flooding my eyes so I could barely see. I did not want my father to go to this strange place called America. I pleaded with him to stay with us but Father explained this was an excellent once in a lifetime opportunity that would better our lives. Mother again held me and told me she loved me and that everything was going to be all right.

Before Father's departure, he made plans for our family and some friends to accompany him to the airport and see him off to this place called America. When we arrived at the airport, father kissed us goodbye. It was an extremely sad moment.

My mind went back to the day of my departure from Jamaica. As I looked at the plane, my thoughts raced back to the big metal bird that I had flown in myself. I looked up to the sky and with my head tilted to one side I said to the clouds, "Lord, Daddy is dead now." As my relatives stood gazing with tears in their eyes, I yelled out, "He's gone, he's gone, Lord, he's gone!" I sadly turned and walked away, with tears streaming down my face. Mother and I made our journey back home and she comforted me as I wept for Father.

Three months passed and Mother and I went to the Embassy to get our visas so we could join my father in America. Within a couple of weeks, the time had come for us to sail on the big luxury cruise ship, Queen Elizabeth II, to America.

On the first day of June, we boarded ship. By the way the passengers were dressed, you would have thought we were boarding that famous ship that sank many years before, the Titanic. This ship was a popular British cruise liner, and Mother had reserved one of the first class cabins for us. We were about to enjoy fourteen days of pure pleasure and excitement.

On the first night of our voyage, the ship ran into boisterous winds and bad weather, which made it unstable. The rolling activity caused almost the entire crew to become seasick. Just about everyone on board became ill. Mother picked up the telephone and summoned help, only to be informed that she would have to wait for quite some time because she was not the only passenger who was sick. Mother was disgusted. However, being a nurse-midwife, she always traveled with her medicine supply. Mother was ready and able to care for both of us, even though she vomited the first few days and I had nosebleeds for the first couple of days.

While on the cruise, there were so many things for us to do. Every morning we would get up, have our baths, get dressed and have breakfast in one of the beautiful dining rooms. We had our very own chef who prepared all of our meals. Only five passengers were seated at our table throughout the entire voyage. After meals, Mother and I walked up to the top deck and went sightseeing.

I always found something interesting to do. The ship had many activities available for children such as a video arcade, finger painting, oil painting, movies, mini golf, dancing and many other activities. On deck were many shops for Mother and I to shop in. During the evenings, after dinner in the luxurious dining hall, there were shows with famous celebrities from all over the world.

I had a lot of fun dressing up every day in all of my best clothes. I felt like a princess in a fairyland storybook. Some days, Mother and I would just sit in the window view lounge and watch the waves as they lashed against the sides of the great ship. The sun radiated warmly on the deep blue ocean water.

The snow-white cotton ball clouds peacefully passed by the ship greeting us on our way as if saying to me, "Hello again, we are still here with you as you continue on your journey." On the fourteenth day of the cruise, Mother and I arrived in a place called New York City.

We passed an enormous tall gray cement looking woman, holding a torch straight up to the sky. Mother asked a ship purser about the statue and was informed that her name was the "Statue of Liberty", which represented freedom for anyone passing by her. It appeared the torch touched those same snow-white cotton ball clouds that I had left behind in England and seen in Jamaica the day I boarded that big silver bird. Those clouds seemed to be following me everywhere I went. They consistently reminded me that I was embarking on the rest of my life and they would never leave or forsake me. They would be with me to protect me for the rest of my life.

After arriving in New York City, Mother's brother, Uncle Keith met us on June 16. We lived with him and his family for five months until it was time for us to reunite with Father. We could not live with him during this time due to lack of accommodations on the campus. You see, Father was living in the dormitories and was on a waiting list for family housing. He had already applied for a family unit and it would not be ready for us until the winter semester.

Time slowly crept by. Finally, winter was upon us and after a number of weeks, Father received a 2-bedroom trailer on campus and left North Dakota to join us in New York. It was now December and we had a beautiful Christmas together. I was excited. We were a family again.

Chapter 8

*I*n January of 1975, we moved to North Dakota, because my father was ready to begin a new semester at the Bible College. By this time, I was almost 11 years old. My parents and I lived in North Dakota for a short period of time. While there, I met many people but only had a few friends who were close to me. During the fall of that year, Father was assigned to a mission on an Indian reservation, in a place called Dunseith, North Dakota.

Every weekend while in Dunseith, I went camping with the Smith family. We had the opportunity to swim and camp outdoors under the blue sky sprinkled with white glistening stars. Every Sunday morning, Father and I drove to the hospital where Mother worked as a nurse, picked her up and then make our 90-mile journey to Dunseith. While at the mission, I met a family who had seven biological children of their own in addition to seven foster children. The mother was a Sioux Indian and the father was a Caucasian man.

Many of the children were quite unruly and they loved to experiment with different things. One of the girls whom I befriended introduced me to my first cigarette. I took a puff of the cigarette and gagged because I was not sure what to do with it. I had a natural reaction. I felt myself gasping for air and began to choke. I wondered if I was to inhale or exhale the smoke. All I knew was to open my mouth and cough. I immediately threw the cigarette on the ground, and decided never to pick up another one again. The experience was too much for me to handle, and I gave it up as quickly as I started.

While attending elementary school, I played the cello and participated in the school choir. Near the end of the school year, the time came for the winter concert. I was chosen to sing the lead for the grand finale song, which was "You Light Up My Life". I will never forget that evening. I was so nervous. As the introduction played, I had just enough time to swallow my saliva, take a deep breath and belt out the first note. I remember closing my eyes and singing "So many nights, I sit by my window, waiting for someone to sing me this song". Even with almost two hundred people present no other sound could be heard in the auditorium. As I neared the end of my rendition, the audience was on their feet. I will never forget the thunderous applause as I closed my mouth and bowed. That was my very first encounter which ushered in a long-standing love affair with music and live performances.

After living in North Dakota for two years, Father graduated from the Bible College and was now ready for graduate school. He applied to a graduate program in Sioux Falls, South Dakota and upon acceptance we were ready to relocate again. My parents sent Grandmother an invitation to come live with us. I was overjoyed because I had not seen my grandmother since I left Jamaica. I felt as if I was on top of the world when the day finally came. I anxiously got up the morning of Grandmother's arrival. After eating breakfast, we took the car ride to the airport. I was glowing. I could not wait to see her.

As we arrived at the airport and parked the car, we walked to the passenger area. I spotted a little brown-skinned woman about 5-ft 3-in tall walking slowly towards us out of the entryway of the plane.

Suddenly my feet felt so light that I took off running down the passageway towards Grandmother. We embraced as we wept in each other's arms and hugged tightly. At that moment, we were not exchanging tears of sadness but tears of gladness and joy. I did not want to let Grandmother go. I felt as if I would hold on to her forever. We made our way back home joyfully, and Grandmother lived with us for two years until it was time for her to relocate to New York to live with her son and his family.

I gave my heart to the Lord at the age of eleven. It was during a Sunday night revival. During this time, my father, as he was a pastor, formed alliances with a couple of local Pentecostal churches in the Sioux Falls area and we supported their ministries regularly. On this particular Sunday evening, I remember sitting in the service and found myself absorbed as the Holy Spirit moved amongst the people and they worshiped and praised God.

All of a sudden, I felt something gently grip my heart and I desired to be saved. I turned to my mother who was sitting beside me in the pew and I told her that I wanted to accept Jesus as my savior. She looked at me and told me to turn around in my seat and kneel down beside her. As I knelt down, my mother told me to repeat some words as she spoke them to me. Thank God for the day He saved me. I believe if I had not given my heart to the Lord, I would have taken another road and not fulfilled the plan God had for my life. God had a plan and a purpose for me and I am grateful that He sealed my heart in my youth.

The next summer as I turned twelve, Father decided to take our family and some friends with their two children to the Black Hills National Park for a week-long vacation. I was excited, because Father told me that I would see the heads of some of the United States Presidents carved out of stone. Grandmother was also going to be joining us on this trip so I was ecstatic.

Once we arrived at the national park, Father's description was nothing compared to what I saw with my own eyes. The sculptures were enormous. I was speechless. The experience was breathtaking. I had never seen such magnificent sculptures in all of my life. I had visited many places in the world, but this left me with a sense of awe and amazement.

During our trip the days were full of fun. My friends and I had the opportunity to swim in the lake, eat hot dogs roasted on the open campfire by day, and then roast marshmallows by the same campfire at night. We bathed outdoors in an open shower stall.

The first night of the trip, my friends, Grandmother, and I slept in a tent. The temperature was about 40 degrees. I was freezing. Boy did I miss my nice warm bed, which was at home waiting for me. Mother and Father ended up sleeping in the car because there was not enough space in the tent for them. They looked like two sardines wrapped together in a can. I laughed at them both as they shivered in the night. I had never seen such a sight like this before. My parents decided enough was enough. We found a motel for the remainder of the trip, and everybody was happy because we were warm and comfortable indoors.

On a Sunday afternoon, a couple of weeks after returning home from summer vacation, sadness clouded our church community where Father was the pastor. Mr. and Mrs. O'Brien had seven children and two of them were a set of 9-year-old identical twins. One particular Sunday, they decided not to come to church because they were going camping instead. Father had preached a few sermons before warning people to be conscious of the activities they engaged in on the Lord's Day. Unfortunately, Mr. and Mrs. O'Brien did not heed the instruction.

While on their camping trip, one of the twins decided he wanted to go off swimming by himself. After about fifteen minutes, the second twin told his mother he was going to swim with his brother. Mrs. O'Brien agreed and off he went.

About two hours passed. Mrs. O'Brien became concerned because the boys had not returned to the campsite. She asked her husband to go and look for the boys. Mr. O'Brien left and was back at the campsite within 20 minutes, this time accompanied by the park ranger, and he looked like he had seen a ghost.

Mrs. O'Brien stopped what she was doing, wondering what had happened. Mr. O'Brien came close to his wife and hugged her with tears in his eyes. She questioned him as to what was wrong, but while sobbing he could not answer. She asked him a second time, "What is wrong?" He responded by saying, "The boys". She asked, "What do you mean the boys?" Mr. O'Brien proceeded through his sobs to tell her that the two boys had been located at one side of the lake holding hands in a 20-foot drop off in the lake. Mrs. O'Brien fainted in her husband's arms after hearing the news.

The park ranger radioed for an emergency team and within minutes, they were all assembled at the campsite with the O'Brien's. Mrs. O'Brien was revived and she let out a cry which could be heard throughout the entire camp. She demanded answers as to what happened to her boys.

After much inconsolable sobbing, the park ranger told the O'Brien's it appeared the twins had gone swimming in a part of the lake that was known for its muddy drop off. By this time, the coroner had been called in, and it was determined the boys had been under water for about twenty minutes.

This was devastating news. Mrs. O'Brien was in a state of shock and amazement and did not know what to do. She felt numb, cold and sick to her stomach. She felt pain in the depths of her soul, like the day she gave birth to the twins. The park ranger escorted them to the place where the boys were. After identifying the bodies, the coroner took the boys back to the town morgue. By the time the O'Brien's made their way back home, they had called the pastor, my father.

After Father heard the news, he told Mother we needed to go to the O'Brien's home to be with them for a while. I became fearful because I did not feel like going to see any dead person or their family. With much regret, I hesitantly got into the car with my parents and we made our way over to the O'Brien's home. As Father parked the car and we proceeded to enter, I felt nauseous. I felt sick and wished that I could go back home. After visiting with the family, and making arrangements for the funeral, my parents and I left their house.

The funeral was Friday morning. Before the service, Father asked me to go with him to open the doors of the church for the funeral home to bring in the caskets. I was scared to death. I did not enjoy this at all. As the two white limousines pulled up to the side of the church, I peeked through the door and saw two small caskets being gently eased out of the cars. I looked around for Father because I did not want to be alone with the caskets.

Father came out of his study to meet the funeral director and the attendants proceeded to carry the caskets into the front entrance and down the long passageway of the church. They lined up the two caskets by the wall and opened them to position the bodies perfectly before the family arrived to view them. I wanted to run out of the church as fast as I could but I did not know where to go. My mind drifted back to my younger days while living in Jamaica, recalling the taunting and teasing of the children as I walked past the cemetery each day after school. I had not faced my demons; fear surrounding death. I did not see the correlation between my early childhood experiences and my present situation as I faced these bodies lying still in their caskets. Before too long, thank God, Mr. and Mrs. O'Brien arrived and entered the door of the church vestibule. This made me feel a little better, because now I was not totally alone.

The boys looked so peaceful, as if they were sleeping. They were dressed in matching white suits. Their jet-black hair was neatly combed, parted and pressed down along the side of their faces. As I compared the two boys, it seemed the freckles were in identical spots on each of their faces, which held slight smiles. They were in their purest innocence at this moment and it just did not seem fair to me. They sure did not seem like the same two boys who only a week earlier were being mischievous and naughty in church.

Fortunately the funeral did not last very long. It was so sad. At the end, their mother wept uncontrollably as she gripped her stomach and bent over each of them to give one last kiss on the top of their foreheads. She finally said good-bye as the mortician closed and locked the caskets for the last time. It seemed as if the whole town had shown up for the funeral. I was relieved once the service was over. All I wanted to do was get out of the church; to forget about the funeral and all of the grief and pain that I had seen, felt and experienced.

As our time in South Dakota progressed, I met more and more friends and enjoyed plenty of outdoor activities. I even had the opportunity to learn horseback riding. I went to summer camp the following year and met many kids. While enjoying a canoe ride with one of my friends named Sue, we made our way to the middle of the lake. We started singing the song "Rock the Boat". Before I knew what was happening, we had successfully tipped the boat over and I felt myself sinking in the water.

I was an average swimmer and did not realize in my panic-stricken state that the lake was not even six feet deep. For a brief moment, I had a flash of the O'Brien twins and pictured myself dying the same way. I fought with all my might because I did not want to drown. After a few moments of regaining my composure, I was determined to fight for my life. I struggled away from the canoe, and began to free myself out of the mud at the bottom of the lake and rose to the top of the water. Within a few seconds, I was floating but coughing and gasping for air. My friend Sue had also fought her way to the top of the water, and was gasping for air. I got out of the water, dragged myself to my cabin and decided to leave the canoeing to someone else. I never went into another boat for the duration of summer camp.

While at camp, I became very popular and won the hearts of many peers. I also met a boy named David. David was a handsome young man, and he liked me just as much as I liked him. David invited me to be his date at the awards banquet, and when he picked me up from my cabin, he surprised me with a sweet first kiss on the cheek. At the banquet, I received the distinction of "Miss Summer Camp" and "Most Athletic Female". It seemed I was quite popular, and recognized. I felt as though I had gained many friends. It was nice because I finally felt validated. After summer camp, David and I corresponded for a while, and then we lost track of each other.

My second experience singing in front of a live audience was at our church in South Dakota. I performed the very first song I'd ever written, called "Spread A Little Love". The words simply said, "Spread a little love, all around you, spread a little love, everyday. Spread a little love all around you. It will brighten up your day, it will help you along the way, so spread a little love today". I can remember practicing a few weeks before my big debut for hours each day. The date of my performance was the most frustrating day of my life.

When the time finally came for me to share my song that Sunday night, I remember sitting at the piano as my father introduced me and shared the title of my song to the congregation. As I opened my mouth for the words and melody to rise from my lips, nothing came out. I literally froze at the piano and could not move a muscle. The silence, which penetrated the church, was unbearable. I wished that I could get up from the piano stool and run out of the sanctuary.

My father stood at the rostrum and simply stared at me, as if saying, I am here for you and whenever you are all set, we are ready to hear you. After what seemed like an eternity, even thou it was only about five minutes, I heard my father say to me, "Sharon, we are ready whenever you are". Talk about ultimate humiliation. I finished singing the song without much effort. The applause from the congregation was amazing. The funny thing is that I did not see that God was preparing me for my future as a contemporary Gospel Recording Artist, even back then.

Within the space of one year, the time had finally come for us to move again. At the same time, the Lord had been dealing with Father about entering into the mission's ministry abroad. Father shared his vision with Mother and I and then moved us to Minnesota for our visas, allowing us to travel to Africa. Mother also continued working as a nurse in the hospital on call. Even though my parents and I lived in Minnesota for a brief time, our stay was pleasant. Father finally got the call from the Embassy and the head office of the church he worked for. We prepared to go oversees and work in a foreign mission. This time we would be going to Liberia in West Africa.

One day, after receiving our documents to leave the country, Father asked if I had adjusted to the idea of going to Africa. I laughed hysterically, trying to hide my fear and told him I did not want to go. All I knew about Africa was what I saw on the television and it was not very appealing to me.

I told Father I refused to live in a mud hut, or walk around town without any clothes on my body. I thought about the images I had seen on television of cannibals eating people and expressed the fact that I did not wish to be eaten by one. Father laughed at me and explained what I saw on TV was not factual. He said Africa was a very civilized place and there were many people from all over the world working in many different fields who resided in Africa. After two additional months of preparation, we were on our way to Liberia.

Chapter 9

*L*iberia is a country located in the western region of Africa. History reveals Liberia is a place possessing rich iron ore deposits with a flat coastal plain that rises in a series of plateaus to a heavily forested interior of low mountains. Many small rivers wind throughout the country. The weather is tropical and humid. Extensive forests contain mahogany, ironwood and rubber trees. Some of the native animals are the pygmy hippopotamus, all species of snakes, elephants, monkeys and buffaloes.

Our flight lasted about 20 hours. When we finally arrived and the flight attendant opened the door of the plane, I felt the unbelievable heat of the air hit me like a 100-degree heater blowing off vapors. It was extremely hot. I was now beginning to experience the differences in temperature and humidity from that of America. With the door of the plane completely opened, a large portable iron staircase was placed against the side of the plane for the passengers to disembark.

As my parents and I descended the squeaky portable steps, I noticed a young impressively dressed black woman waiting off to the left of the airstrip for our arrival. As we descended the stairs she waved while waiting patiently to take us to our destination. Once on the ground, we entered the small airport to claim our bags and were ushered into the taxicab and off to our new adventure.

To my surprise, as we made our way from the small airport downtown through the city and into the town where we were going to live, I spotted hundreds and hundreds of people hustling and bustling with market goods on top of their heads and on carts. People were everywhere, and there were so many black people. So many children were poorly dressed; bare-footed with extended stomachs. I saw many variations of people; from light-skinned, dark, to even in-between colored people. I recall the same expressive stares we received in Scotland were the same ones these people had. This was a new experience for me because they all were of dark complexion, just like me. However, as time would unfold, I found the answer to this focused observation.

As we continued driving through the overcrowded streets of the capital city, Monrovia, a very distinct odor enveloped my nose. Whew! It hit me in a hard way. Wow, I would never forget that smell. Garbage and sewage was everywhere in the streets. The level of poverty and sewage was overwhelming.

The street vendors were everywhere. Dirty water overflowed onto the streets from the sewage drains, running in all directions. I saw a man facing the wall as he urinated without any shame. I thought to myself, how disgusting this sight was. I felt my stomach turn upside down. I saw a woman walking on the street with a pan on her head. In the pan appeared to be a blackened fist looking thing. When I questioned Father, he said it was monkey meat in the pan. I shrieked with horror and we soon left the city streets.

I began to see enormous, beautifully gated and magnificently built homes. I saw luxury cars parked in front of well-manicured lawns, artistically landscaped. I did see a few mud hut homes on the side of the road intermingled between these fine homes, but they were rare. I saw women and children wearing uniquely colored wrap skirts and sandals on their feet. The women were carrying huge baskets on their heads filled with produce either just bought from the market or on its way to be sold. I even saw some women that were naked on their upper bodies. Their breasts were just swaying in the wind in total freedom. It was so funny to see this. I began to laugh to myself. I also heard many unfamiliar noises. Chirping sounds in the air were strange to me and I could not recognize them.

After about 30 minutes, our taxicab made a turn into a long driveway positioned off the main road. As I looked out the window of the car, I beheld a beautiful home poised behind a high-gated wall. It seemed as if it was on an acre corner lot. Women peddlers sat against the wall of the house selling freshly peeled oranges and other fruits and vegetables. This seemed strange to me. No one bothered the women as they sold their produce. As I looked around my surroundings a little more keenly, I saw other women selling fresh fish, breadfruits, mangos and a variety of other products. I wondered to myself if these women had licenses to sell their products as we did in America.

A huge church was located just a few feet from the high wall. Hut homes made from mud and straw sat on the property located just outside the gate of the house. A mother had her baby swaddled to her back in a type of cloth wrap as she bent over an outdoor wood fire, cooking the evening's dinner for her family.

The taxicab pulled up to the front of the gate and it opened. As the driver proceeded to stop under the covered patio, a man came from inside the house to meet the car. After holding the door open for us, he further proceeded to bring the luggage inside. One thing I observed was when he got to the steps of the side door, he removed his slippers, wiped his feet, and then went inside the house barefoot. I was baffled.

The woman who picked us up at the airport was a missionary from England. She had been sent to Liberia to work with my father. She introduced herself as Sister Livingston as she smiled at me. She said ever so politely "Hello Miss Sharon!" I was speechless. Why did this woman call me Miss Sharon? I curiously responded, "Hi!"

Sister Livingston then proceeded to take me by the hand for a tour around the house. It was about 3,000 square feet. The entire house had white, marble tiled floors. The large sitting room had mahogany wood furnishings with blue velvet. Houseplants were everywhere. I peeked into the four oversized bedrooms with four large full-sized bathrooms. The large immaculate kitchen contained every possible customized appliance. In the large laundry room was a modern electric washer and electric dryer. This was the most beautiful 4-bedroom house I had seen in a while. It looked like a mansion. My parents and I had house workers that took care of us, 24 hours a day and 7 days of the week.

While looking around the house, I thought I saw something move on the wall. I blinked twice, and looked at the wall again. To my amazement, I saw a little white creeping creature glide across the wall. I let out a scream because I was not sure what it was I saw. Once I regained my composure, I realized it was an innocent little lizard. These were quite common in African homes. I hurriedly turned around and headed in the direction of my parents. In my haste, I realized my arm was bleeding slightly. I had scraped my wrist on the corner of the wall as I ran away from the lizard. This scar would remain on my arm and in my sub-consciousness for the rest of my life. I prayed I would be leaving this place called Africa very soon.

The people in this town had the same physical features as me but they were different in the sense that the indigenous population, or those who were considered the poorer class, was utilized in the homes of the affluent as house servants. These people were responsible for washing our clothes and cleaning the house.

For us, there was no such a thing as equality; they were subservient. This made me very sad. They were not to hold conversations with my parents or me. Their wage compensation was equivalent to a meal consisting of some rice, fish and palm oil, or whatever food was available. The injustice and inequality given these people made me very angry and I did not want any part of it.

I often wondered why injustice was so prevalent amongst them. The very thought of this practice caused me to cry because I could not comprehend why these people were being treated differently from others. It was inconceivable for the helpers in our home to address us by our first names at any time. I was Miss Sharon. This was a culturally appropriate attitude for demonstrating respect. It was incomprehensible for me to imagine as a thirteen year-old girl acknowledged as "Miss" by someone two or three times my age.

My first few weeks of settling into Monrovia were interesting. I recall one day my mother and I took the local mini bus into town. As we waited at the bus stop, I looked around my immediate surroundings and noticed some schoolchildren intensely checking me out. As I gazed at these inquisitive children, I noticed them looking at my feet. I had on socks up to my knees and nice shoes. I was shocked at their display of awe.

I looked at their feet. Even though they were dressed in matching school uniforms, they did not have socks on at all and their shoes were worn down, unlike mine. I began to chuckle within myself at their amazement as they looked at me and smiled. Even thou we looked alike; they knew I was not like them. They knew I was not one of them, that I was a foreigner from a strange country. What a lesson for me to learn. As time progressed on, I learned how to adjust my dressing so I would not draw attention to myself in an attempt to blend in with the local native people. Although, as much as I tried to be like them, I never quite fit in.

The workers told me I could not share any personal information about myself, such as my age, birth date, or any other thing about myself to the people in our community. The reason behind this was to disclose personal information about my family would expose us to a superstitious belief called "voodoo", or black magic; in other words, witchcraft and evil.

Legacy has it that some people in Africa practiced a different religion other than what my parents and I practiced. Legacy even says certain people would take the information shared with them and try to hurt people with curses and tricks. This bit of knowledge made me extremely scared. I am convinced it exposed me to a sense of unknown fear. From that day, I was very careful not to hold personal conversations with anyone outside of my immediate circle.

Mother was able to continue her nursing practices with the women in the interior villages by educating them and helping them with their infants and children. Hundreds of children came to see her in the clinic from various villages on a daily basis. Mothers brought their newborn babies so that "Ma", as they called her, could take care of them and place her blessing on each and every one of them. Mother took regular trips into the interior for those women who were unable to find transportation into town. She delivered their babies, took care of the sick children, and taught the women how to be homemakers and good wives to their husbands. She taught many of them the basic steps in recognizing different symptoms of many common illnesses arising in their children, and how to treat them.

One unforgettably beautiful and sunny Friday afternoon, while playing by myself in the yard with my dog Rudy, there arose a sudden sound of singing and rejoicing resonating from the streets. As my curiosity peaked and I became attuned to what was about to unfold around me, I climbed up to the top of the wall. I saw about 20 young girls in a processional, dancing as if in a school marching band. Leading the march was a man dressed in a native costume. It appeared he was demonstrating a tribal dance while chanting some unfamiliar words.

He was gracefully twisting and twirling in every direction with the timely beat of the drums. He seemed so intent; focused and in deep concentration. Immediately following the leader was a group of women, who probably were the team leaders for the girls. They chanted all types of words and sayings in their dialect. They were making different funny sounds, whooping and hollering at the top of their lungs. Legend says this was a ceremonial dance to their supreme deity. The atmosphere at that moment felt dark and the presence of evil was evident.

The town's people came out from every area of Painesville to view the processional. They were cheering and clapping for the girls as they passed by. The girls were all dressed in native colored tie-dye wrap skirts and their upper torsos were exposed, revealing their breasts. Their upper bodies were beautifully sculptured with a type of white paint, which covered them from their heads to their waists.

After a while, the processional disappeared. The music faded away and it was all over. No one could explain where the group went. Legend had it that these girls were going through their rites of passage and were attending a type of school where upon graduation they would come out into society as women. The girls in the parade appeared to be around 12 years of age. Some say the custom was to give a sacrificial offering, so one of the girls possibly would not come out of the school because she would be presented as the actual sacrifice.

As I thought to myself about what I had just seen, I appreciated my culture, because my mind could not comprehend the very thought of experiencing this type of process just to declare my woman-hood. The thought caused my body to shiver and my blood ran cold. If this tale was true, I considered the question in my mind, what if I was the girl chosen to be the sacrifice for the day? My body again shivered and I quickly removed myself from the wall and went back to playing with my dog.

While living in Liberia, I attended the American Co-op School. It had a mixture of all cultures and nationalities of children. The teachers were all from America. I was 13 years old now and in the 7th grade. One of the classes I had to complete was home economics. Since there were no current educational materials available for progression, I ended up having to take the same class two semesters in a row. It really did not bother me too much. Overall, I was able to keep up with the American curriculum; therefore, I dealt with the barriers and excelled in my studies.

We had now lived in Africa for about six months. One afternoon as I arrived home from school, I entered the house and had a sense that something was seriously wrong. As I went into my father's room to greet him, Mother met me and she was crying. Father was gravely sick, almost at the point of death. Father had contracted a severe case of malaria and was running a dangerously high fever. I had never seen my father sick like this before. As I neared the bed where the doctor was attending to him, I felt a sense of nervousness. My mind reflected back to my friend Lillieth and losing her to a terrible illness. I did not want to lose him in the same manner so I began to pray to God to heal my father and not take him away.

I became overwhelmed with a sense of sadness and fear. The tears collected in the corners of my eyes and rolled down my face as I looked at him. I did not know if he would live or die. I looked across the room at the bed where he lay and gazed directly into his eyes as he affectionately looked into mine. The smell of sickness overwhelmed the air and I felt a sensation of pain settle in the pit of my stomach. I approached the bedside, gently took my father's hand and told him that I loved him.

I could see the pain in Father's eyes. I closed my eyes, and prayed again and asked the Lord Jesus to heal my father, and not to take him from us. I told God everybody I loved or cared about had left me or died, and I could not make it if he took my father. I promised if He allowed my father to live, I would be good and not be a nuisance to my parents. I told God "Thank You", laid my father's hand back down by his side, and walked out of the room. Later that evening, a car arrived to take Father to the hospital. I got in the car with Mother and we rushed through the city to the small private hospital run by American missionaries on the outskirts of town. The ride lasted for about thirty minutes and I used the time to reflect on how much I loved my parents.

As we arrived at the hospital, Father was escorted into a room and we waited until the doctor came and attended to him. An IV was inserted into his arm and an oxygen mask was placed on his face. He was not talking to us because of the pain medications given to make him comfortable.

After the doctor examined Father carefully, he was given additional medications then released to recuperate at home. We served him fresh fruits and nourishing meals daily. Each day after school, I spent valuable time with Father as he progressed, looking stronger and stronger. I made homemade cards and hung them on the wall for him to see, which made him smile.

Within a few days, Father began showing significant signs of improvement. By the fifth day, Father was able to sit up in the bed and hold conversations with us. He was returning to his normal and healthy self. We took Father back to the hospital for a follow-up examination and he was finally given a clean bill of health. In a matter of days, he was able to take brief walks around the compound for daily exercise.

A short time after Father's recovery from malaria, we prepared to take a trip into the interior village where some of the native church people lived. It was necessary for my father to go into the inner most areas of the villages to meet with the people because he held such an important role as an overseer and Bible school principal. He went to see how they were living and to assist in any way necessary.

This trip was to be an extra special one because Mother and I were going along with him. As we made our way to the car, Father briefed us on what things we could do and what we could not. One of the things which could not be done was using the people's toilet facilities simply because there was no inside plumbing. In other words, there were no public toilets.

I was mortified. How was I going to handle this situation? I had never used the outdoors as a bathroom before. I was stuck. Father told us we would have to use either a leaf or a piece of newspaper discretely behind the bushes. I thought I was going to die. This also meant I would have to limit my intake of foods and fluids. I thought in my mind that if I could change my mind about going, now was a good time to do so. Father also told me that I could not wonder off anywhere by myself.

During our visit there was a story circulating in one of the villages. A woman had delivered a baby and someone who did not like the woman put a spell on her baby and caused it to die. also It was said the day the infant died, the father laid it outside on a bundle of dried branches with the intention of burning the child's body; but by the time preparations for burial were completed, the baby had disappeared into thin air. After hearing one of the natives sharing this story with my parents, I found myself inching closer to my father and mother for safety. I made sure that I did not leave their sight. The trip to the interior was an unforgettably adventurous one for our family.

The women taught Mother and I how to braid our hair in the many African styles. My hair was plaited and so was Mother's. We both looked so beautiful after our new hairdos were completed. I was tickled and just beside myself.

It was amazing for me to see how the people lived and worked, and even how the children played amongst themselves. The mothers performed daily chores with infants tied securely to their backs in a piece of cloth. Some of the women did not wear anything on their upper bodies. Their breasts seem to lose elasticity; they were so flat and elongated, reaching all the way down to their belly buttons. These observations caused me to laugh to myself, because I had never witnessed anything like this before. These women appeared to have no sense of shame or disapproval about their bodies. Everyone in the village respected them. Their bodies did not seem to be the focus of attention, it was all a normal part of their cultural behavior, and it was acceptable.

I observed the children running around the village carefree and innocent; chasing each other with a piece of stick, not worrying about anything. They were genuinely happy; enjoying each other and playing games with stones, rocks, and dirt. They had never experienced the luxuries of television or video games. They had never even seen a picture of a bicycle or skateboard.

I recall before leaving America to come to Africa, Father and Mother told me they were selling my skateboard and ten-speed bike because we could not take it with us. I was so upset and disappointed at the time, because those two pieces of my personal possessions were quite dear to me. Now as I focused on the children who had never seen a skateboard nor bike and probably would not care if they had one or not, I realized how insignificant my skateboard and bike were. The fact that my parents could purchase these toys for me at any time became of no importance to me. I wished I could have given all of those children a bike, a skateboard, or a television set. Even a radio would have sufficed.

I immediately felt a deep sense of sadness for the little boys and girls as I noticed the way they were poorly dressed. They had striped tops with holes to go with the faded, spotted bottoms. Most of them had no shoes on their feet. I realized how blessed and fortunate I was. I was thankful.

As I observed the younger children, some of their bellies were bloated; like inflated balloons ready for a party, because of malnutrition and worms. They had malaria and other types of diseases. Lack of appropriate medical care was a major problem. These children suffered from malnutrition and hunger because they were not fortunate to have three square meals per day plus complete, wholesome and nutritious snacks. Junk foods like potato chips and cookies were luxuries never experienced by these children, and as I realized what these children did not have, it made me very sad. I thought about how I could choose what I wanted to eat and when I wanted to eat. I could even discard and waste food without ever thinking about it. I felt guilty. The children's hair was uncombed and they had no shoes on their feet. My soul went into a state of humility and gratefulness. I wished I could take the entire village of children home with me. I wanted to clothe and feed them all but knew I could not.

Their houses were built out of mud and other natural resources. The roofs were aluminum; there were no brick houses with beautiful roofs in the interior. When the rain fell, it made wonderful music as it tapped in synchrony on the rooftops.

The inside of the houses were not carpeted, but natural dirt. No thermostats controlled the heat or the air conditioning temperature. The hot houses had no fans to cool them. The only item visible was a thin straw mat neatly placed on the ground in the corner. The brooms used to sweep the house were hand crafted with straw by the women of the village. They did not have beds with wire frames or insulated and padded box springs and mattresses. The homemade beds were intricately crafted by the men of the village from oak trees in the forest and the thinly weaved blankets that covered the beds were made by the hands of the women.

They had no refrigerators to keep the food cool. The men and boys of the village hunted for food on a daily basis. The women dug in the ground for foods such as yam and potato, and also picked fresh fruits like green bananas, mangoes, papaya, oranges and breadfruit, along with other vegetation from the herb trees and plantation. A freshly killed chicken or some other meat, like monkey, snake, or whatever other animal could be caught, was the main entree for the day's meal. The women sat on a stool with a wooden bowl between their legs and a martyr stick, which was used for pounding the cassava root to make flour. A soulful and melodious tune could be heard resonating from the depths of the women's bellies as they rhythmically pounded the sticks into the bowl. It sounded like sweet music to my ears. I relished the experience.

At night, we slept in the Village Chief's home and the best provisions were shared with us. Even though we did not have nice comfortable beds to sleep in, padded mats were placed on the ground for us. We slept in our clothes and tidied ourselves with the simple one-stream shower hoses provided for us. The temperature remained quite humid and hot during the nights so we did not experience the effect of coldness as we slept.

Our meals were made fresh every day and only the chief's wives prepared them for us. The local chickens gave us fresh eggs and the pigs provided the meat for our protein portion. We ate papaya picked from the tree. The women picked breadfruit and roasted them in the open fire. The men dug yams from the ground of rich soil, which were then peeled and boiled along with the green banana picked fresh from the tree. We were well nourished and cared for while we lived with the village people.

My parents and I stayed in the villages for two weeks at a time, and then it was time to return home. As we made our journey back, Mother decided to stop for a picnic at the largest rubber tree plantation park in the world. The trees were enormous in size. I could hear the hissing of the wild animals and birds in the trees. Even though it was a bit scary to me, it was peaceful and tranquil to the rest of the family.

Sunday mornings were enjoyable for me because I went to the headquarter church where my father was the pastor. The church was a very large one, hosting about 500 people each Sunday. I was afforded the opportunity to sing during the services, which I loved, yet I looked forward to the services for one main reason. A musician attended our church that played the guitar and sang very well. He was a fine looking light-skinned young man and a soldier in the military army. I had a secret crush on him and looked forward to seeing him every week. I could not reveal my feelings as it was dangerous for anyone to be seen speaking publicly with a soldier, and it was much more dangerous for me as a foreigner.

I was not concerned with being unable to communicate with him, so I kept my feelings alive inside, hoping for the day when I would be able to share them. The one opportunity I had was our common interest in music. We often played music together in the church and I was content with even the brief interaction between the two of us.

It was a Friday, about 9:00am on a beautiful spring day. My parents and I awoke to the sound of commotion and immense shouting outside. Horns were honking and the echo of gunshots whizzed through the air. I was terrified because I did not know what was going on. Mother came into my room and quickly pulled me out of my bed. She whisked me into her bedroom and under the bed for safety from the flying bullets.

After the noise and commotion stopped, my parents and I removed ourselves from underneath the bed and ran to the windows, peeking to see what was going on outside. One of the house servants ran up to the house, banging on the door. "Pa, Pa! Ma, Ma! Open up the door! The President is dead! The President is dead!" Father opened the door and let the man inside.

He was gasping for air, his eyes blood-shot with fear. He looked at Father and told him the President was dead. Father ran to the radio and turned it on to see if he could hear exactly what was happening.

The news reporter stated rebels had seized the palace and assassinated the President of the country. The rebels minced his body into pieces and had it on display for the public to come and see. My parents and I were terrified. We proceeded to get dressed for the day and Father told Mother that we should go into town to get some groceries and provisions to last for a few days, because we were not sure when things would return to normal.

We waited for a few hours until the excitement seemed to diminish. Later that day, Mother and I caught a bus to downtown Monrovia. Father felt it best to stay at home to assess the extent of the damage to the compound and to see if any of our church people had suffered loss or devastation.

As we proceeded on our way to board the bus for our ride into town, we saw and heard a great amount of celebration and excitement all around us by the local townspeople as they lined the streets. Soldiers were everywhere. They had guns positioned on their shoulders trying to keep the peace in and around town. People were running around frantically. I did not know what was going on, but I sensed something was terribly wrong.

Mother and I went into the supermarket only to find the store in utter chaos. Food items were thrown all over the floor. The wet goods were mixing with the dry goods. Milk was blending with orange juice, rice was mixing with crackers, and the volume of food crunching under people's feet as they stepped on the fallen goods intensified. People were stealing from everywhere. The shopkeepers stood back in amazement and shock, not really knowing what to do to protect their goods and property. The townspeople were shouting and screaming at the top of their lungs. It was totally an uncontrollable scene.

As Mother and I left the supermarket with our few items, we attempted to flag down a bus, leaving town back to Painesville. The approaching bus came to a stop, and we proceeded to get on. As we stepped up into the bus, I felt the tight squeeze from my mother's hand become significantly tighter. This made my heart beat faster.

As I looked into the faces of the people seated on the bus, the only language they expressed was one of fear of the unknown.

While Mother and I took our seats in the middle section of the bus next to a soldier with his gun pointing up to the sky, it began to rain. The rain of tropical countries was not the rain I was accustomed to in America. These raindrops seemed to be the size of dimes falling uncontrollably from the windows of heaven. The sound of the rain intensified as it made contact with the bus. Within about 10 minutes, the rain was pounding so hard it sounded like the beating of a thousand sticks on a thousand bass drums.

All of a sudden, as the bus turned the corner, there was a loud "boom". The bus swerved out of control and finally came to a complete halt. All the passengers tossed like clothes tumbling out of control in a dryer. Once we composed ourselves, we all looked around and rushed off the bus. I saw what was left of a young soldier whose body had made impact with the back of the bus. His body was lifeless and his head was shattered into a million pieces as fragments of flesh lay scattered everywhere on the ground.

I looked at what was left of him and I noticed his complexion was darker than the soldier boy I had fallen in love with. I was relieved. This soldier was a stranger to me. The young man was dead. The smell of death and raw blood rose in the air. His rich red blood had blended with the rain and flowed everywhere on the ground. It splattered all over the bright orange-yellow bus and his bike lay in mangled pieces off to the side of the road. A group of women immediately united in a loud wailing chorus and started a high-pitched mourning chant. They chanted louder and louder, and within a short period, the chanters grew in number.

Mother grabbed my hand and pressed forward through the crowd, we then crossed the street to the other side of the road. I saw some men who were riding with us on the bus scrape the remains of the dead man and toss his disfigured body parts and mangled bike into the back of a pickup truck. I later learned the reason for the crowd's shouting was the bus driver allowed his friend to drive the bus while he lay in the front seat taking a nap. The friend thought he could jump ahead of the oncoming soldier riding on his bike and misjudged in turning the corner. As a result the back of the bus hit the soldier's bike. He fell and became flattened like a broken pancake in a dry skillet within a matter of seconds. The camera of my mind captivated this incident and memorialized it that day, and it will remain there always.

After witnessing such a horrific incident, Mother flagged down a taxi. She and I squeezed in with five other persons into a very small 4-door taxi and made our way home to Painesville. Attempting to get back to the house was an extraordinarily challenging feat because the bullets continued to whiz by our ears. As the taxi came to our stop, we exited hurriedly while the bullets continued sailing through the air. Mother and I quickly grabbed our few grocery bags and dodged into the house for safety.

As we entered the front door, Father informed us that the news of the President's murder, along with some of his cabinet men, was true. His assassins had cut the body into many pieces and his remains were shown on television, left in the middle of downtown Monrovia for public display. I felt sick to my stomach. I was so scared. All I kept thinking about at that moment was the fact that I wanted to go back home to America, where it was safe. I thought to myself this was no place for me as a 14-year-old teenager to grow up.

My parents and I returned to the safety of hiding under the kitchen table for cover from the bullets that flew through the air over our heads. For the first few days after the coup, we ate food sparingly, mostly non-perishable items. For the first time in my life, Mother fed us food without seasoning, uncooked and cold because we had to ration our food to make it to last as long as possible.

By the end of the week, my parents and I received word via telegram from our headquarters church in Tennessee that we would be leaving Africa; that is, Mother and I would be going back to America without Father. Later that Friday evening, an announcement came over the radio that the American President was flying all American women and children out of Liberia for safety. All American men had to remain because the rebels would not allow them to leave the country. That meant my father would have to stay behind which made me very unhappy and I began to cry.

The Monday morning before Mother and I flew out of Liberia, the local news station showed a picture of the beach where six telephone poles were positioned. On the poles were six men bound and tied. The image was similar to when Jesus and the two thieves were crucified on the cross.

Each of the men had a black bag placed over his head. Military soldiers shot them dead, one by one, on command. After they shot those six men, they continued to bind and tie other men to the telephone poles and shot them dead. These were some of the remaining cabinet men of the dead president. Oh such bloodshed!

The man that took over the presidency was a soldier not more than nineteen years old. People say he could neither read nor write. Someone said after he assassinated the President, he then brutally shot the President's daughter to death. Oh the bloodshed, heartless and without mercy!

Later that week Mother and I were at home packing for the journey home to America. All of a sudden, there was a loud knock on the door. Father went to the door and to his surprise were four armed soldiers. Mother and I were so scared, because we did not know what the soldiers wanted.

After a few minutes Father shut the door, walking slowly as though in a state of shock, and came back to talk to us. He told us the soldiers were looking for a man who was a part of the ex-president's cabinet and they wanted to know if Father had seen him. They were looking for the man to kill him as they had done the rest of the men on the beach.

The next morning, while my parents and I were eating breakfast, the sound of gunshots echoed outside the kitchen window. We all dived from the kitchen table to the floor. Our breakfast along with the dishes flew in every direction. Sounds of shrieking and yelling were heard loudly outside the yard. After about 45 minutes of chaotic noise, there was an eerie silence. Father got out from under the kitchen table first and discretely peeked out of the window to see what was going on outside. He saw a crowd of people gathering by the church wall.

Father instructed us to stay under the table while he attempted to go outside of the house. Within minutes, Father came back into the house. The look on his face was one of fear and terror. Mother asked what happened, and he responded with fear in his voice as the tears rolled down his face. He said Joseph, the young man who worked in the house with us, and two other men were dead for no apparent reason. The soldiers had opened fire and shot people randomly. Blood was everywhere. Joseph had a wife and two children, a four-year-old boy and a two-year-old girl. Mother and I were so sad that we broke down and cried. Again, I wished at that very moment that I could go straight to the airport, get on the airplane and go home to America. I wanted to go home and the departure day could not come soon enough for me!

Shortly after that shooting, about a week before Mother and I were to leave Liberia, we were fast asleep about 3:00am in the morning when a loud scream penetrated the stillness of the night. "A Rogue! A Rogue!" Everyone was startled. Now, my dog Rudy was a full-bred German shepherd, and it seemed strange that she did not bark. Of course, no one could go back to sleep.

The commotion was due to a thief that had oiled himself down with petroleum jelly, climbed up the side of our house naked, and attempted to make his entrance into the house from the crawl space in the roof. Before he did his mischief, he fed Rudy some poisonous food, which put her to sleep. Later that morning when my parents and I went outside, we found Rudy frothing and foaming at the mouth. Father decided to take her into town to the vet's clinic. The veterinary doctor told him Rudy was too sick and needed to be put to sleep.

When Father came back from the vet, there was a great commotion outside on the yard. About 50 people congregated together. My parents and I went out onto the veranda to see what was going on. In the middle of the highly charged and tightly knit crowd, was the thief! The crowd was aggressively beating the young man to death with sticks and rocks, for his crime of attempting to break into our house. Apparently, this was not the first time he had committed such a crime, and his deeds had finally caught up with him. The custom of the village was if you were a thief and got caught in your wrongdoing, you would be beaten to death, or the part of your body used to do the crime would be cut off. I again thought to myself, what an unforgettable experience for a young foreign girl.

Chapter 10

*T*he time finally arrived for Mother and I to leave Africa. Days seemed like weeks, months, and years. I was so excited and overflowing with joy to be leaving Monrovia; yet to leave my father overwhelmed me with mixed emotions.

I woke up that morning feeling as if I were on my way to freedom; no more bloodshed, no more fear. Wow, what a glorious day! Once again, we were flying on that big silver bird with the long wide wings. I was not afraid this time. I was ecstatic to be leaving.

I was afforded the once in a lifetime opportunity to experience Liberia as a young girl for a particular reason. While in the midst of my journey, I never saw the lessons being taught; of gratefulness, appreciation, humility and compassion. I learned to appreciate the simple things of life. I realized how blessed and fortunate I was as an American girl. Before going to Africa, I took many things for granted. I was selfish, and self absorbed.

I left as a new and empowered person. I was educated in the principles of life and appreciation. I developed a sense of mission and empathy for those less fortunate than I. I did not realize my mission in life was being intricately weaved into the fibers of my character as a teenager. I will always be grateful for my African journey.

As I hugged Father and bade him goodbye, I began my ascension up the steps to the inside of the plane. With those same tears in my eyes as the day I left Jamaica, I looked up to the sky and the clouds seemed to be saying, "You are about to enter the next phase of your life. We will never leave you nor forsake you." With sadness overwhelming my heart, I attempted to comfort myself as I found my seat and looked out the window searching for my father. Our eyes met and we both waved goodbye for the last time.

After what seemed to be a never-ending flight, Mother and I arrived in New York City. We passed that tall cement-looking woman, holding her torch up to the sky. For us the Statue of Liberty again represented freedom, but this time in a significantly special and meaningful way. I observed those snow-white cotton ball clouds touching the torch and I felt she was saying to me, "Welcome back to freedom".

Mother and I spent a short time with Uncle Keith once more. After staying with him for two weeks, we made the trip to New Jersey, where preparations were underway for my guardianship with a new family. I was placed with them because I was yet a minor, only fifteen at this time, and not old enough to live by myself. Mother could not stay with me in America because she had to return to Africa and continue the mission work.

One particular occasion while staying with a friend of my family in New York, I was sexually abused. My mother and the older family members went on an outing. The man who molested me stayed behind to supervise the children that evening. His wife had gone to work; you see she worked nights as a nurse in the hospital.

It was about 8:00 in the evening. He told all of the kids to go into the living room to lie down on the floor and watch TV. However, he invited me to sit beside him on the sofa. He turned out all of the lights. The room was in utter darkness except for the light that came from the TV.

I was the eldest of all the kids and without thinking did as he asked. I was taught to obey my elders, so I did not question his request. While we were watching the television, he snuggled up closer to me and put his arm around my shoulders. I paid attention to his breathing as it increased quite heavily and made me feel very uncomfortable.

He placed his free hand on my lap and attempted to draw my skirt up to my thighs. He asked if he could give me a kiss on my cheek, and I said no. He forced a kiss anyway. The sound of keys was suddenly heard at the front door. He quickly removed his hand from around me, fixed himself and moved over to the other side of the sofa, pretending as if nothing was going on.

Thank God his wife came into the living room and greeted us. Within a few more minutes, my relative returned to pick us up. I was relieved because the abuse stopped; just in time. I realized if the family had not returned home when they had, my abuser would have raped me. I felt sick to my stomach and confused. I did not feel at ease within myself because I knew this man would have violated me, if given the opportunity.

I let out a sigh of relief and since that day, I never laid eyes on that man again, nor did I tell anyone about my ordeal, and I was glad. I hid that experience deep in the core of my soul for protection from exposure and shame.

Chapter 11

*A*fter settling in with my new family, Mother rejoined Father in Africa and I stayed behind to start my life again. My new family had children and we embraced each other. By this time, I had attended seventeen schools from elementary to high school; some of them for only one week. I experienced all types of schools; from public to private, even Catholic.

A major problem began to surface in my life. I found myself feeling very lonely and isolated. I could not figure out why I was experiencing these particular feelings. I always felt as if I did not fit in anywhere. An indescribable void was in my heart because, until this time in my life, I had never experienced such loneliness, sadness and disappointment. To be honest, if these feelings were present in my soul, I had never allowed them to surface into my mind and become a significant part of my consciousness.

I found myself angry many times. I was confused and felt alone, unloved and unwanted. My mind reflected back on the incident in New York with the stranger who molested me and I felt sorry for myself. I felt violated as a young woman and did not understand why I was experiencing these uncomfortable emotions.

For the first time in my life, I began to question who I was and where I came from. I knew I was adopted by my parents whom I loved ever so deeply, but I felt there was more to me than who I was at that present moment. I began to notice a secret desire surfacing from within my heart to meet my biological father. My soul yearned for something that I could not explain.

I was experiencing feelings of emptiness and darkness. I had a large black hole inside my heart, which hurt so terribly. I knew something was missing and if I met my biological father, perhaps the void and bad feelings would somehow disappear. I did not have the same void for my biological mother, and that seemed strange. I never questioned it, I just focused on him. I think I was angrier with her for giving me up for adoption than anything else.

I knew something was wrong and did not know where to begin. I trusted no one, especially men. I had been hurt and let down by different men in my life, and I had no confidence or trust in them. I felt wounded, bruised and rejected, wondering perhaps if I was a mistake or an unfortunate accident.

I also was experiencing a fear of attachment to people, because deep down inside, I really was not quite sure who I was as a person or where I had come from. Even though I knew my parents loved me unconditionally, I could not connect with those feelings at that time. I just felt hopeless and obsolete.

I felt if I allowed myself to become close to anyone, I would be hurt or in jeopardy of them leaving me. I was afraid to develop a relationship with anyone because of the probability of having to leave them and move away. To my surprise, I remained at my new home up until I fell in love and married the man of my dreams.

The first few months of settling into my new home went well; I was superficially happy. Even though I received enormous amounts of love and attention, it was not enough for me.

My life was constantly filled with unending activity. Singing became an integral part of my life. I was very busy in the youth and music department of my church. I helped with the choir, and we even had a singing group. Our choir met weekly for rehearsals and every weekend we were invited to churches all over New York, New Jersey, and Connecticut. The young people always had something to do.

Our house was the focal meeting place for the youth group of our church. Even though we all had a strong bond as a youth family, I was attracted to one particular young man in the group who was quite popular with all the girls. The thought of us developing a relationship was inconceivable simply because as a youth group, we associated more as a family than anything else. I was not dating anyone at the time and I was not looking for a boyfriend. I focused on my books and felt a boyfriend would be a distraction and cause nothing but trouble.

I did not consider myself an unattractive girl. I ran track and field so my body was in excellent shape and my curves were well defined. I only weighed about 120 pounds and I was five foot six. I had shoulder length black hair and even though my self-esteem was not great, I enjoyed looking good. This was just the way Mother had taught me to present myself publicly.

He and I shared many commonalities. Most of us in the group had a love of music and this young man did as well. Within a brief period, we became good friends and I trusted him unconditionally.

One Saturday night during a typical sleepover with a group of the young people, while everyone else was sleeping, I felt the nudge of the young man as he gently awoke me. He whispered in my ear that he wanted to talk to me about something very important. Half asleep, I threw off the sheets, got up out of my bed and went into the den to talk with him.

All of a sudden, he had one hand over my mouth so that I could not scream very loud and his other hand was around the back of my neck. Before I knew what was happening, he forced himself onto me. With all his strength, and with a good fight from me, he shoved me into the bedroom where the other boys were fast asleep, seemingly unconscious to the world. He shut the door and threw me onto the area where he slept. After much resistance from me, he forced himself onto me and violated me as he ripped my womanhood away.

I suffered during this unforgettable act, and after much struggle, I finally was able to free myself from his grip. As I escaped from the room, I cried and cried, running into my room where the other girls were yet fast asleep. As the emotions and hot tears welled up inside I sobbed uncontrollably because I hurt so badly.

I woke one of the girls named Penny, who was wrapped up snug in her sleeping bag also dead to the world, and shared what had just happened to me. She tried to console me and then we locked the room door as she did her best to encourage me to lie down until morning. After much contemplation and inner turmoil, I consented to lie down in bed until I cried myself to sleep.

I found myself wounded and broken for many days after that fateful incident; physically, emotionally and spiritually. I was embarrassed because I thought everybody knew what happened to me.

I became reclusive and stayed to myself, determining if anything like this ever were to happen to me again, I would rather die than live through such a nightmare. I shared my secret with one of my friends and deep inside my soul learned how to endure the pain and the shame. I felt dirty. I felt shame and embarrassment towards my self.

I never told my family, nor did I write my parents in Africa to tell them what happened to me. I just kept the horrible secret to myself as it gradually tore at my heart like a cancer. I would see the young man frequently; at school and at my home during different occasions. He would look at me and smile as I turned my head in the opposite direction, not wanting to look at him. Every time I saw him, I felt nauseous. I just wanted to throw up.

About a month after the ordeal, I began to pray because I needed a way out. I cried out to God for help. I did not want to be in this situation any longer. I was unhappy and missing my parents who were still in Africa. I wanted to meet my biological father, and it seemed that nothing good was coming my way. My life felt like a total train wreck. I wished for God to rescue me from my torment. I knew God was the only one who could give me hope and strength to make it. I was successful in keeping this secret even from my guardian parents, simply because I didn't want to let anyone know how much I was hurting or the true depth of my sadness and lack of self-esteem.

From that day on for about a year he would frequent the house, pretending to visit with my family, just to taunt me. He even tried to befriend me; always apologizing for his behavior. He never missed an opportunity to be with me, and I did everything in my power to avoid him. I took his sincerity lightly because I was not interested in his advances anymore and I could not bring myself to forgive him for what he had done.

My self-esteem had hit the floor and fell beneath it. I never really made any new friends for the remainder of my high school years. I did not even feel worthy enough to have friends. I believed I would never amount to anything. I felt that dreams belonged to other people and not me. I believed I would never find the happiness I so desperately desired. The only safe place for me was my quiet time in prayer and meditation. I prayed a lot. I enjoyed listening to gospel music and it was in these private times that I found peace. This was my therapy, my medication.

I do not know why I never entertained the thought of turning to drugs or alcohol to mask the pain. The last thing on my mind was to abuse my body or allow myself to be involved in negative relationships. I did everything within my power to avoid these types of situations because I had a sense about myself and I was determined to live and not die. Now I understand God was not keeping me against my will, but rather He was preparing me for a time when I would share my painful story to encourage others in their place of despair. Later on in my life He would strengthen me through my own experience to let others know they are worth believing in; no matter what situations challenge their lives, they are to live and not die.

I realized an unexplainable desire and determination in the depth of my soul that would not allow me to give up on life. I wanted to succeed and never let go of my dreams or desires. I accepted the fact that something bigger than me was in control of my life. Even though I could not see the full panoramic view of my purpose in life, I sincerely believed all my experiences were a part of my development into the person I was meant to be. I learned how to depend on God. I learned how to communicate with God and I felt

Him communicating with me. He helped me and kept me emotionally intact. I found inner strength and the ability to keep smiling even though I still had more trials to come.

On another occasion, we were having a graduation celebration at my house and many of the same friends had been invited. During the party, my friends and I were sitting in the basement, and he came into the basement with his friends. As I saw him coming down the stairs, I felt an uneasy feeling welling up from the pit of my stomach and told my friends I needed to become invisible. They encouraged me not to leave and said they would handle him if he even tried to bother me. He approached us and I immediately got up from the area where we were sitting and went into another room pretending to use the telephone.

He followed behind us, pushed my friends out of the way, and threw me down on the sofa. He then invited his friends to jump on top of me. I found myself face down on the sofa as they jumped on top of me like someone stacking pancakes onto a plate, all the while laughing as if it were a funny joke. The pressure was enormous and it was quite difficult for me to breathe. I felt my breath leaving my body. I thought I was going to pass out. I closed my eyes and prayed, hoping God would deliver me. I could not yell. I could not scream. I could not utter a word, because I was under so much pressure.

My friends immediately collected themselves, turned around, saw the young men piling on top of me, and shouted at them, demanding they stop and leave me alone. They ignored my friends, until they began beating the boys vehemently with their fists. They finally decided to get up, yet laughing, and walked out of the room. The boys were ordered to leave immediately.

I was again broken. Another part of my heart had fallen off. I felt so stupid and handicapped. Why was this happening to me again? Why was he being so mean to me? Angry, I ran into my room, crying hysterically.

I could not believe what was happening. All I knew to do was ask myself the question, why this? Enough was enough! After running upstairs, I finally decided to tell my guardians about everything he did to me.

They called the young man and his parents on the telephone to discuss what happened and to inform him if he ever bothered me again, he would find himself in a lot of trouble. He apologized and agreed to not bother me anymore. The taunting and embarrassment ceased; however, in a short space of time, the physical abuse would continue.

From my birth up until this time, I had never experienced being in a hospital as a patient. I became inquisitive as to what it felt like to be in a hospital. One summer during my seventeenth year of life, I noticed what seemed to be a small bunion on my toe. In my naive state, I thought it was a blister and picked at it. I then began having pain in my right foot.

I went to the doctor and after taking a battery of tests, he said I had a growth and needed surgery to remove it. He was not sure if it was benign or cancerous, thus the surgery would remove the growth and allow him to rule out any further problems. Early Wednesday morning, by six o'clock, I was on my way to the hospital. The surgery only lasted one hour and then I was sent to the recovery area to awaken from the anesthesia.

By that afternoon, I was settled into my room. I was very lonely because I had no visitors. The whole ordeal was a strange one because to this day, I do not understand why any of my friends did not know I was in the hospital. I was solely by myself for the first couple of days. Boy, I wished someone would come to visit me, but no one came.

After being in the hospital for three days, my guardians called to say they would be visiting that afternoon. I was ecstatic. They asked if I needed anything. I thought for a moment then answered I would take a tuna sandwich. I was not really supposed to eat any regular food yet, because the IV was still in my hand, and I was receiving antibiotics and pain medication. I did not care. At that time, I thought what the hospital staff did not know would not kill them, not realizing how it could affect me. I was hungry and tired of hospital food and I needed some real home cooked food. When my family arrived, I rose up from my bed with joy and propped myself up with pillows to eat my sandwich. Within five minutes I had devoured the entire sandwich and was satisfied, or so I thought.

After their visit, I began feeling nauseous and a sharp pain shot across my abdomen. I let out a sound. The pain attacked me again and I wondered what in the world was happening to me.

Before I could process what was going on inside my body, I had an enormous urge to use the bedpan. I could not hold myself together. My bowels moved and within seconds, I felt a warm sensation coming from my back part. I had to use the bathroom, and I could not contain myself. I moved my bowels all in the bed and had messed all over my bed sheets. I was humiliated. I had to call the nurse, because I could not walk to the bathroom by my self. I did not want the nurse to figure out what I had done to cause this embarrassment.

Before discharging me from the hospital, my doctor advised I needed to rest at home. He instructed me to use the crutches and keep my foot elevated to reduce the pain and swelling. My family members were at work, so one of my friends picked me up from the hospital and took me home.

Again my tormentor came to my house because he had somehow heard I was coming home from the hospital, and decided to pay a visit. We pulled up into the driveway and he spotted us from the window. As he saw me coming towards the back door, he slammed it right in my face, refusing to let me into the house. Since we couldn't get in through the back door, my friend and I had to wait outside until he finally decided to let us inside. My foot was throbbing. The pain was so intense, and I was hurting badly. I again felt worthless and alone. All I could do was break down and cry.

The house had multiple levels, therefore, I planned to stay on the first level to lie down and relax. However, once inside, he brought in his two dogs, and let them loose on both of us. He irritated the dogs so that they would be cross enough to bite me. I hopped as fast as I could with all of my might across the room to avoid them. My friend helped me shuffle quickly through the kitchen straight into the bedroom and slammed the door as we locked our selves in the room and prayed. We prayed for him to recapture the dogs, take them outside, and that he would leave and not come back. After the ordeal, he left and I was able to relax until the family returned home from work.

The last incident with this boy, which broke the camel's back, was the day my friends and I were at the house down in the basement. He and some of his friends were visiting, as we all congregated as a group on a regular basis. The guys all participated in sports activities together and they were practicing for a game. He approached me and started swinging some sticks in my direction, attempting to hit me in my face. After a split second, I realized what he was trying to do and got up from where I was sitting and tried to dodge his attacks.

He caught me and handcuffed both of my hands tightly behind my back onto a cement pole in the center of the basement. He was highly amused and began laughing hysterically while I cried. As both his friends and mine begged him to give up the key, he ignored their pleas and brushed them off. After about fifteen minutes, he finally unlocked the handcuffs and released me. Thank God, the ordeal was over.

Again, I prayed for courage and a way out. I was afraid of him and needed God to listen to me. As I re-live this incident, I see correlations between this boy and the children who used to taunt me in Jamaica, and even with Peter, the little boy in England who taunted me as a child. Why was I unable to stand up for myself? Why was it so difficult for me to fight back? I wished I could board a plane and go back to my parents in Liberia.

In spite of all I experienced, I never shared any of those ordeals with my parents because I did not want them to worry about me. I was a good student and did very well academically in spite of the abuse. On the other hand, my social life left much room for advancement.

At the beginning of my senior year in high school, I received a letter from my father informing me he was coming to America and wanted to take me on a shopping spree. When Father arrived at the airport, he took a taxi to the house. I heard a car door slam in the driveway. As I looked out of the window, I saw my father exiting the taxi.

I was overjoyed. I loved my father dearly and missed him ever so much. I raced through the house, out the front door, hurdling the three cement steps and fell right into my father's open arms. I wept tears of joy as Father hugged and kissed me. I felt within myself that everything was going to be all right now. I knew nothing or no one could hurt me anymore because I was with my father. All of the loneliness and pain was temporarily forgotten and I was happy.

Within a couple of days, because of the closeness of our relationship, Father noticed I was acting somewhat withdrawn and reclusive. He suspected that something was wrong. We spent the entire day shopping in downtown Newark, and after visiting a few stores and buying some things, we were famished. He took me to lunch, and we had a wonderful time. We saw a little Chinese restaurant on the corner and decided to stop and eat there.

I had shrimp fried rice and chicken wings and Father had chicken lo mein and broccoli beef. The meal was good and our conversation was enjoyable. Halfway into the meal, Father put down his fork as he looked straight into my eyes and asked how I had been doing. He asked if everything was alright with me. I swallowed my last forkful of rice and dropped my eyes as I looked down into the plate and told him yes. By the response I had given, he knew I was not telling the entire truth. Father did not push me to talk, because he knew eventually I would let him know all that I was feeling. I really wanted to tell him the truth. I wanted him to go over to the boy who had repeatedly hurt me and rough handle him just as he had done to me, but I decided not to tell him.

This is how I viewed the situation: if that boy did not change his ways, the horrible seeds he had sown into my life might someday be reaped back into his own life. I did not wish bad things to happen to him but I wanted him to understand the torment he inflicted made me unhappy and uncomfortable. Father and I changed the subject and continued our conversation for about another hour, and then we left the restaurant to continue our shopping. Father stayed at my guardian's home for two weeks and then he returned to Africa and my mother. When the day finally arrived for his departure, I was very sad because I did not want him to leave. While he was with me, I felt safe and secure. I also had someone I could talk to that understood and really cared about me.

That summer, I graduated from high school with high honors in the top one percent of my class. Even though I had done well academically, I was not happy about my accomplishments. I felt I had no reason to celebrate. I did not feel as if I had accomplished anything major in my life. It was not a big deal for me; it was just graduating from high school. I missed my parents and was sad because they could not attend my graduation ceremony. I wished that they might have been there to see me receive my diploma and to celebrate with me.

Not only was I not happy with my accomplishments, I was very unhappy inside. One might ask, why did I have such a dominant sense of not belonging anywhere? My answer is I did not know who I was. I was tired of the abuse, and found myself living a life full of secrets, pain, and disappointment. I was looking for a place to plant some roots and I could not find it. I was searching for a love I felt was unreachable. I wanted someone to love me for who I was. I wanted to be complete.

I do not blame my parents for any of the adverse experiences that happened to me. Neither do I blame my guardians, because for a young woman my age, I was one of the most fortunate human beings alive. I had traveled the world and experienced probably what many of my peers never would in their entire lifetime. I remained prayerful and continued to ask God to send me a friend; a true friend who would respect and love me for who I was, not use and abuse me. I continued to pray this prayer and stayed to myself. In spite of all I had gone through, I did not even realize those trials were all for my making for the future. I would not find this out until I married and began having children of my own.

Since our church was involved in many singing engagements all over the New York/New Jersey tri-city area, we came in contact with lots of young people along the way. This is how I met a particular young man, one might say, my first real boyfriend. His name was Barry and he was a sailor in the United States Navy. The correlation to this piece of the story and my future husband might not be clear at this time, but as time will reveal, there was a connection between the two of them.

Barry was a church boy and he was four years older than I. He would call daily and visit my house regularly. Our relationship began to grow. Over a period of time, we became close and he fell in love with me, but I really did not love him. He was interested in moving forward with the relationship quickly. Barry was preparing to go overseas for military duty and had plans for us to be married. He was an aggressive young man, but this approach seemed quite unattractive to me. He wanted to become engaged to me, but I was not ready for that kind of a commitment.

On a Sunday afternoon, a group of young people was hanging out in the front of the church while waiting for services to begin. As I looked off in the distance, I noticed a car pulling up. I focused in on the car and the occupants inside. The two people were, at that time, my best friend and her brother. As I paid close attention to her brother, it was love at first sight. I recall saying out loud, "I must meet that man." The young man was tall; he was dark and ever so handsome. Wow! My eyes had never beheld anyone so beautiful in my entire life. He was perfect and I needed an opportunity to meet this beautiful human being. I could not wait for church to be over. That evening the youth choir was to perform in White Plains, New York at a church program. As soon as I got home from church, I asked my sister if she thought I should call my friend to get an opportunity to speak to her brother. She encouraged me to make the call.

I proceeded to call my friend and asked if I could speak to her brother. She gave him the phone and I froze on the other end of the line. I immediately regained my composure and said hello, he responded on the other end of the line. I introduced myself and asked a few questions about him. Unbelievably, it was easy to talk to this young man. I looked up at the clock and realized we had been talking on the phone for over two hours. I ended up inviting him to the concert that night and he agreed to attend.

As soon as I hung up the phone with Donovan, I immediately made a call to Barry informing him that I had met someone. I told him I was not interested in talking to him anymore; I wished him the best for his life and hung up the phone.

Donovan met me at the van, which was taking us to New York, and we sat together. I was attracted to his glasses. They seemed so dark and mysterious and made him seem ever the more attractive. While at the concert, after our group performed, Donovan and I decided to take a walk and talk about life and become better acquainted with each other.

We talked about many things and learned we had so much in common. Before we realized, the time had come for us to take the three-hour trip back to New Jersey. When we got home, we called each other and spoke briefly before saying good night and going to sleep.

The next morning could not come fast enough for either of us. Keep in mind, Donovan was in the Navy preparing to leave that

Monday for boot camp. Monday came too soon, but we promised to keep in correspondence with each other. I wrote the first letter and I did not hear anything back for a couple of weeks. I wrote him a second letter and finally received his first one.

We continued corresponding. Donovan graduated from boot camp and then deployed to Japan. I was sad to see him leave, but we promised to keep in touch while he was away. Over time, our relationship grew and I knew that one day he was going to be my husband. I had prayed for a friend just like Donovan; however, I didn't see at the time that God was blessing me with a double bonus by also providing me with the man who was to be my soul mate. Donovan was my knight in shining armor, the prince in my story.

Chapter 12

*A*fter graduating from high school, I continued to live with my guardians and began attending Rutgers University in Newark for the upcoming fall semester of 1982. One day after contemplating about my biological father, I decided to contact my Uncle Baz who also lived in New York. I learned that he and my biological father had been best friends in Jamaica as children. My uncle also knew where he lived. I spoke with my uncle and shared my need and desire to meet my biological father.

My uncle agreed and said he would do his best to find my father, talk with him, and try to convince him to meet me. He promised to get back in touch with me as soon as he had some definite information. As promised, within three months time, he got back to me. Unfortunately, he informed me that my biological father did not want to meet me and wished to be left alone. That was the end of that, or so I thought. Deep inside my heart, I felt it was not the end for me. When I hung up the phone with my uncle, I felt as if someone had taken a knife and pierced me in the deepest and darkest part of my heart. It was such an indescribable pain and agony; I did not know what to do with myself. The tears flowed uncontrollably and I cried for what seemed a lifetime, but in reality, it was only days.

Every time I thought about what my uncle had said to me, it made me feel worse. All I could do for the moment was push my thoughts and feelings deeper into my soul. Those feelings of abandonment returned even stronger; of not being validated or wanted, with a lack of love and total hopelessness. I found myself so miserable and unhappy.

One day I went to God in prayer, asking Him that before I closed my eyes in death, to please allow me to meet my biological father. With that prayer, I left it alone.

Music was a vital part of my life at this time. Not only was I a member of the Rutgers concert choir, I also took voice lessons, sight reading and vocal dictation classes. I met a young man by the name of Rodney who was a well-known pianist throughout New Jersey and a music instructor at the school. The first few weeks of my freshman year, Rodney and I practiced singing and one day, he dropped a bombshell announcement: I was going to be performing for the incoming freshman students at the welcome reception hosted by the school.

I was so nervous. The song I was to sing that day was "Wake Up Everybody". Rodney and I practiced for hours and then it was time for me to perform in front of 300 students. Rodney began to play the introduction and I recall opening my mouth and closing my eyes to sing. About halfway through the song, I opened my eyes to look out into the audience and forgot the rest of the words. I learned very quickly how to adlib on my feet. I will never forget the look of astonishment on Rodney's face as I glided my way through the rest of the song. When I finished we received an outstanding ovation. Of course, no one knew the words I sang were not the actual lyrics, but we pulled it off perfectly.

I remember Rodney patting me on my back and saying, "Girl, you are good!" I will never forget that experience. I learned such a valuable lesson that when I am in the spotlight I have two choices, either sink or swim, and I chose to swim.

While experiencing all my new transitions in college, I decided it was time to meet my biological mother, Miss G, who was still living in Jamaica. I contacted my grandmother in New York and invited her to return to Jamaica with me. I made the flight reservations and Donovan paid for my ticket. Grandmother would be flying out of New York and I would be flying out of New Jersey. We agreed that once I collected my luggage, I would just wait for her to arrive. Within a few weeks of making plans to go to Jamaica, we were on our way.

I was so excited because I was not sure what type of person Miss G would turn out to be. The last time she had seen me was during my first six years of life. As my plane landed in Montego Bay, I felt a sense of excitement and anticipation for what was about to take place in my life.

I exited the plane and did my best to pick Miss G out of the crowd of people who had gathered in the passenger pickup area. I spotted a woman who had similar features as me. Of course, my grandmother would recognize her right away. However, her flight had not arrived yet so I was on my own. I had to search just for a brief second and suddenly I saw her off in the distance.

Her face was round like mine, she had the same skin tone as me, and she was tall in stature like me. I was overjoyed. As we approached closer we stopped and stood in front of each other for a moment then hugged. I looked into her face and I could see she had the widest smile. I also noticed three young men who seemed to be between the ages of twelve and sixteen years of age standing beside her. They were her sons, my brothers.

As Miss G and I embraced each other, they came closer towards us and embraced me warmly as well. We stood in a tight huddle briefly as we embraced and just looked into each other's faces with excitement and anticipation. I looked at her and asked what name would be appropriate for her, and she responded, "Call me what ever makes you comfortable". This is where the name Miss G originated.

I picked up my luggage and we all proceeded to the lounge to wait for my grandmother's flight to arrive. Within three hours time, her plane landed and we went to greet her. Again we embraced each other, exited the airport and then entered a van that had been waiting for us. We then proceeded to make our way to Miss G's home in the town of Montego Bay. After settling in, Miss G and the boys prepared a meal and we ate together as we continued to get better acquainted with each other. Miss G had a man living with her and the boys, which was a unique situation for me, but I did my best to overlook this minor technicality.

We spent our days touring the island and visiting various tourist attractions throughout Jamaica. One day while we all were at the house, there was a knock at the front door. As one of my brothers opened the door, a young man stood asking for me. My brother let him into the house, and he approached me saying he was Earl's son and his name was Arthur.

I felt quite uncomfortable because too many new challenges were being placed upon me at a rapid pace. Who was this person identifying himself as my brother? I had no prior knowledge of Earl having any other children. I embraced him on the surface because I did not want to disrespect Miss G or the boys. I observed her reception towards this young man, which seemed quite passive. Arthur visited with us for a few hours and then he left. He lived in Savanna-la-Mar and I did not talk to him again until fate brought us back together later in life.

My grandmother and I spent two weeks with Miss G and my younger brothers. I felt it was a good time for me to visit my aunt in Kingston as my grandmother went into Savanna-la-Mar to visit her sister for a week. My youngest brother Val and I boarded one of those mini buses to Kingston, which was a five-hour drive from Montego Bay, to see Aunt Marie who was now a teacher.

We had a wonderful time in Kingston, taking a boat ride to the famous and historical Port Royal. We visited the Botanical Garden Park and many other tourist attractions. We even had an opportunity to visit my aunt's church for a couple of services.

At the end of that week I was now ready to return to Montego Bay because my grandmother would also be returning from her visit with her sister to take me back up to Darliston. This would allow me to see my birthplace and visit with some of the old-time residents who knew me as a small child.

Unfortunately, as I made my way back to Montego Bay to Miss G's home, I returned to an uncomfortable situation where my belief system and Miss G's belief system did not agree on certain issues. I felt the best thing for me was to end my trip early and return home to America.

I did not want to disrespect Miss G, so instead of being in a situation that made me uncomfortable, I felt it best to fly out of Montego Bay one week earlier than my expected departure. When my grandmother came back to Montego Bay, Miss G informed her I had returned home just a few days earlier. Of course my grandmother was disappointed because she was prepared to take me around to all of the people who knew me as a child. I was later told the people of Darliston had planned a big celebration for me and I was sad that I had to end my trip prematurely.

At the end of the third week, my grandmother flew back to America. She called me once she returned home to New York and inquired as to the reason for my early departure. I shared with her that there were certain principles of which I disagreed when pertaining to Miss G and my brothers.

I felt that before I disrespected her, it would be wise for me to return to my world where I did not have to tolerate such contradictions to my belief system. After leaving Jamaica, Miss G, the boys and I kept in touch by writing letters to each other for quite some time and then the communication tapered off somewhat.

I attended Rutgers University NCAS for three years, telling myself I wanted to be a nurse. I was taking a twenty-one-credit course load. I had chemistry, biology, college algebra, English, history, and a voice class. Not understanding the real contributor to my problems, I began to burn out. I went crazy. I crashed academically and ended up withdrawing myself completely from school. I applied for a job at St. Vincent's Nursing hospital and began to bury myself in work. I worked all the time, every shift, as much as I could possibly stand. During all this, my relationship with Donovan remained constant and we grew even closer.

On one of Donovan's brief visits home, while in my second year of college at the age of nineteen, he surprised me with an engagement ring that was designed in Japan. He proposed and engaged me that December during the Christmas holiday. I had not yet received the blessings of my parents, but I was not worried because I knew in my heart that I was going to marry this man one day. As we courted over the next couple of years, we wrote at least once a week. I would send Donovan tapes of me singing and talking to him. I just believed these thoughtful deeds would help to keep him encouraged until he finally came home from his tour of duty.

Each time Donovan came home for brief visits, we spent valuable time together, dreaming and planning our future together. The common vein that kept us together was our similar interests, hopes, dreams and goals. We desired the same things in life. He wanted a house and I wanted a house. He wanted four children and I wanted four children. We took many strolls up into the affluent sections of East Orange and admired the beautiful mansions and landscaped yards. We definitely agreed with each other (Amos 3:3). I believe that God gave us to each other as a special gift.

Only one barrier seemed to keep us challenged in our relationship, and it pertained to our religious beliefs. You see, Donovan was raised from a child as a Pentecostal, the same as I. However, because his parents migrated to America from Jamaica, his grandfather (who was a Seventh-day Adventist) raised him during his teenage years. This was of great concern to my parents and they thought the relationship might not work because of this barrier. Once Donovan completed his tour of duty, he came home and remained faithful to the religious teachings of the Adventist faith. I also remained faithful to my religious teaching in the Pentecostal faith, and nothing could move either of us from our convictions, or so we thought.

Donovan finally decided to write my parents, asking for my hand in marriage, and they responded to him by saying no directly. They expressed to him that after I graduated from college would be the appropriate time for me to think about marriage. Donovan sent me the response letter from my parents and asked what I was going to do. I told him that come what may, I was determined to marry him. I desired the blessing of my parents deep within my heart. I would not have felt at peace without it.

As time went by, my parents returned to America for a furlough and we spent an entire night convincing my parents why I knew Donovan was to be my husband and all the reasons why I needed to marry this man. Towards the break of day, my father gave me his blessing and I began to plan for my wedding. Donovan came out of full duty with the Navy after four years and enrolled in school to obtain his degree in Aeronautics. He completed a two-year program and was hired during a job fair. His new employer was so gracious that they held his position for about three months, enabling him to graduate before sending him to California to work. Through all this, God was working in our lives and orchestrating the full plan which He chose not to reveal to either of us, simply because it was not yet time for revelation in its fullness.

Graduation from Teterboro School of Aeronautics came in November of 1984 and Donovan was on his way to California. While at work one day, Donovan met a man by the name of Deacon Waugh who became a dear friend. Deacon Waugh invited him to service one Sunday at a Pentecostal church. After the service, Donovan called me in New Jersey and was so excited. He shared that he had gone to one of "my type" of church service. I was so excited for him. This church was where God had planned for us to become a family and play an intricate part in the ministry.

Plans for our wedding were coming together nicely and the closer our special day came into being, the more excited we were. Selecting the colors for the wedding was exciting. We chose pastel summer colors; lavender, teal green and pink, with my maid of honor wearing pastel peach. Then we searched for flowers, rings, invitations and all the other important components of a wedding. We also had the daunting task of choosing the photographer, the musician, the cake maker and deciding who was going to play what part in the wedding. All these 101 things thankfully finalized before the actual wedding day. Slowly but surely, all the plans came together with just a few days left before the time came for us to walk down the isle as husband and wife.

Our wedding day was beautiful. It was a Saturday and the sky was blue and full of those cotton ball clouds that started out with me when I lived in Jamaica as a child. I was truly happy. I had found happiness and peace and I was in love with the man of my dreams. Two hundred guests were invited and Aunt Marie and Grandmother played intricate parts. Aunt Marie was a bridesmaid and Grandmother made all of the bridesmaid's dresses and the maid of honor's dress. Donovan and I were not fortunate to have a honeymoon because he had only been with his new job for six months and had not accrued any vacation time. I was still working at the nursing home so all I needed to do was submit my two-week resignation letter.

That morning my maid of honor took charge of everything, allowing me to have a stress-free day. I woke up about nine o'clock in the morning and took a long and relaxing bath. After eating breakfast, it was time for me to have my hair done then return to the house. The photographer was scheduled to meet us at noon and by the time we arrived, he was patiently waiting in his car. I went quickly inside the house and proceeded to get dressed.

By one o'clock, we were ready for the photographer and began taking pictures. All six of the bridesmaids and two flower girls showed up for the photography session. We took a host of pictures and then it was time to go to the church in Montclair, New Jersey. Two o'clock came and one white limousine pulled up to the front of the house for the bridesmaids and one Bentley for me. I had always dreamt of riding in a Bentley for my wedding and I remember having to take brown paper bag lunches to work for one year in order to save up the four hundred and fifty dollars enabling me to pay for the cost of the car. I felt a sense of pride as my father and I sat in the car because I knew I was living my fairytale, a Cinderella dream wedding.

The wedding was set to begin at three o'clock in the afternoon. As we proceeded to the church, we took the forty-five minute drive from East Orange to the church in Montclair. Guests were already arriving for our grand occasion. The church was decorated with so many beautiful flowers, bows, and mixture of guests. The center isle was long and set the perfect tone. As I exited the car, I was quickly ushered into the waiting area of the church.

Suddenly someone came and told us one of my attendants had forgotten her bouquet back at my house, forty-five minutes away, so one of my friends decided to drive back to pick up the flowers.

My maid of honor suggested we go back into the car to keep me relaxed because I was feeling a sense of anger and disappointment rise up in my heart. The limousine driver suggested taking us on a little site-seeing tour. We got lost and could not find our way back to the church. After about forty-five minutes, we made it back to the church. The time was now about four o'clock in the afternoon. After my friend returned with the flowers we finally proceeded with the ceremony at 4:30pm.

I sang the song "You and I" to Donovan and he was ever so nervous. You could hear sniffles and people blowing their nose as I sang. Finally, we were pronounced husband and wife and went on to the reception. We spent our wedding night in a quaint hotel on Route 22. The next morning, which was Sunday, our parents held a family brunch and finally we were off to the next chapter of our journey. We left our family with lots of hugs and kisses and my guardian drove us to the airport for our flight to California. The odd paradox was that even though I was happy and in love with my new husband, I found myself weeping for the entire five-hour flight to San Francisco. I really do not know why the tears were flowing. Perhaps subconsciously I was saying good-bye to the past as Sharon Williams and finding closure and completion as I prepared to embrace my new future as Sharon Jones.

Nevertheless, the tears seemed uncontrollable for me. Donovan did all he could to comfort me. Before we knew it, we were finally in California and moving into our apartment, ready to begin our new lives. Our first year of marriage was wonderful and we lived the "American Dream".

Despite my apparent contentment and happiness, there seemed to be a sense of emptiness brewing underneath the surface, for whatever reason. I could not understand why because everything in my life was going well. I was truly happy and in love but the feeling that something was still missing hovered over me. That dark hole seemed to be overtaking my heart and I was unsuccessful in figuring out what was going on deep in the core of my being. I lacked confidence within myself. I did not realize I possessed God-given gifts and talents. I had forgotten how to believe in myself and I was troubled.

Within two and a half years of our marriage, we were ready for our first child. The pregnancy was pleasant. At the end of my forty weeks, our little J'eannine decided to make her entrance into the world. J'eannine weighed in at eight pounds ten ounces, and she was our bundle of joy. My husband and I continued enjoying our marriage and my new role as a mother. I loved my daughter and Donovan and I were happy. Our lives were complete.

From my daughter's birth until she turned two years old, I nursed her and was a stay-at-home mom. I nursed all of my four children for two years each. However, breastfeeding during the mid-1980's was not a popular practice for a lot of mothers. Compounding the problem was that I was a young black woman who nursed my child exclusively.

I remember many occasions of people staring as I nursed my daughter while shopping, as if I had committed an unforgivable sin. If I was in the grocery store, I had to abandon the cart and leave my items hidden in a corner, while I sat in a hot or cold car (depending on the weather) to nurse my daughter. I would then return to the store, hoping my groceries were left untouched to complete my shopping. That seemingly simple trip would take hours to complete, leaving me exhausted once I returned home.

I recall one particular occasion when my husband and I were eating at a nice restaurant. The waiter approached our table and asked me to stop breastfeeding my daughter because it was inappropriate and unacceptable. I was shocked and disgusted. I excused myself from the table and proceeded to the ladies room to continue nursing her.

The public bathroom was filthy. I entered one of the stalls and leaned against the wall with my foot propped up to hold my daughter because I refused to sit on the filthy commode. While standing there in the public toilet feeding my daughter, I was saddened and thought to myself how unfortunate it was. I did not eat my food while at the toilet, so why should I subject my daughter to those conditions? I was infuriated and began to cry. In public places like church, I had to excuse myself from the occasion or service just to feed my daughter because I was too embarrassed to breastfeed publicly.

The incident which broke the camel's back occurred while flying first class to visit my parents who were staying in Cleveland, Tennessee on furlough from the Africa Mission field. I was the only woman; the only black woman with a baby who was about to breastfeed amongst a section filled with white business men.

As the plane departed from the gate, I decided to feed J'eannine to prevent her ears from popping due to the air pressure. The stewardess approached and asked if I needed anything to drink. I had covered J'eannine with a baby shawl, so I had my privacy somewhat as I nursed her. All of a sudden, J'eannine decided to yank the shawl from off my shoulder and expose both of us to the world. I was so embarrassed.

That day on the plane, I decided to create some type of garment which would allow me to have my privacy and at the same time nurse my child in public. I remember praying to God and asking Him to give me an idea for a product which would allow me to both feed my baby publicly and also offer privacy while doing so. I could not wait to get back to California. When we returned home a week later, I took a crib sheet and cut it into a diamond-shaped cloth. As I continued to analyze and experiment with the fabric, the idea came to me: why not put two rectangle pieces of cloth or two receiving blankets together, cut a half moon in each one, attach velcro to the pieces to provide closure, and create two flaps in the front as a viewing pocket? Believe it or not, it worked!

One nursing shawl took about six hours to create and sew by hand, and I enjoyed making them. At this time, it was early 1988. I wore my shawls in public and people took notice. I started getting requests to purchase my shawls, which made me realize I had something important on my hands. I thought about patenting the product, but procrastinated with the idea for no particular reason. By the time J'eannine was two years old, our second child was on the way. We named him Donovan Jr.

For about two and a half years, I continued sewing and selling my shawls. Initially I made them by hand, but then I purchased my first sewing machine and was able to make them in about two hours. In 1991 after the birth of our second son, David, I decided to investigate having my shawl patented. Unfortunately, in my procrastination from 1988 to 1991, a woman in Kansas patented her own nursing shawl which was somewhat different from mine.

While I was busy being a mother, Donovan was busy working and settling into his new job. Within six years, he was offered the opportunity of relocating to Florida, which was closer to his family. We left California in November of 1992, the same weekend that Hurricane Andrew struck South Florida. I did not realize then how the transition of that move would impact my life's journey in an unforgettable way.

After four months, our last child D'anthony was born at South Miami Hospital. While living in Florida, we attended Macedonia Church of God in Christ. I decided to pursue having my nursing shawl patented and asked the Assistant Pastor, Elder Chadwick, to pray for me and consecrate my patent application package. I gave the package to him on Sunday and the following Friday I received a call that I could come and pick it up.

I arrived at his home excited and anxious to hear "the word from the Lord" given to Elder Chadwick. Upon my arrival, I was met at the door by his wife. She handed me the package and said good-bye without one word from him. I just stood at the door for a moment while collecting myself from the disappointment.

That Sunday, my family made our way to church. After Sunday school, Elder Chadwick beckoned me to speak with him during the break before morning worship. What he shared brought tears to my eyes. He prophesied into my life and revealed that God had a work for me to do. The whole time, I thought he would prophesy about my shawl, but he did not. He said what God had in store for me was beyond my wildest dreams; if I knew what God had for me, I would shout right then and there. He also shared that God would not give what He had for me all at once, but would instead reveal and demonstrate the gifts piece by piece. Had He given it to me all at once, I could not have handled it.

From that day and for a few years afterwards, I was tempted to call Elder Chadwick and ask for particulars. The Holy Spirit told me to leave it alone. I can now say I understand why. After seven attempts over a five year period, the patent office denied the requests to register my shawl. I was disappointed, but I realize had I received the patent, I would have missed my destiny. Perhaps, I would have been manufacturing and selling baby products instead of fulfilling the mission God had set for me.

Chapter 13

*M*y marriage was unbelievably happy because I had the husband of my dreams. We loved each other dearly. We were blessed with four beautiful children. We were economically established with money in the bank. We had purchased a three-bedroom home within the first year of our marriage, bought our first brand new automobile and settled as a family into our new expanded lifestyle.

After spending four years in Florida, the Lord began working on preparations for us to return to California. At the time, my husband and I did not realize this was a major preparation for our ministry. Donovan applied for a transfer with his job and then it was time for me to do the same for mine with the Veteran's Administration where I worked as a ward clerk. Within three months of my husband's return to California, I received my transfer and the children and I were on our way back to begin the next phase of our journey.

Once settled in our new home, I felt a strong desire to open my own business selling my nursing shawls to other women. I researched the idea and learned a lot about becoming a business owner. After completing the necessary paper work, I received my business license and was ready to open shop.

My first location was in my garage. I obtained a business permit and hired three of my friends, Deborah, Robert and Curee to assist with sewing and we did quite well. After a few months, I decided to research the available retail options in the market. I made hundreds of calls to different companies trying to sell my nursing shawls, including a company named Marshall Fields located in Minneapolis, Minnesota. After convincing the sales rep that I had a brilliant new invention, my husband, the children and I were on a plane to Minneapolis to showcase my shawls.

I was so excited. I didn't have much knowledge, but I obtained experience through on-the-job training, that is, learning as I worked. With my son and shawl in hand, I proceeded to my 9'oclock appointment with the buyer for the presentation. By the end of our meeting the buyer agreed to purchase six shawls. I was to return home, fill out the PO and ship them to the store for market testing. I was too embarrassed to admit I had no idea what a PO (purchase order) was. As I look back on the experience, I realize how much I learned which helped me to be where I am today.

Unfortunately, upon our return to California, the economy took a downward turn and the project was placed on hold. The experience was priceless. After that initial encounter, I decided to expand my business and my husband encouraged me to transition from the garage to a public building. I researched the opportunity and decided I needed a loan in order to expand my business.

I applied for a business loan and was rejected by every bank simply because I was a new business owner who lacked sufficient business credibility. I recall approaching at least five different banks only to receive the same treatment at each of them. The response, "You need at least two years of established business ownership" will always be embedded in my mind. I recall one of the last banks I approached, looking at the business consultant after being rejected again. I told him, "I will be back and when I do come back, it won't be to obtain a loan, but to take money out of my own account." I remember him chuckling and saying to me, "Mrs. Jones, I really believe you".

After going through the growing pains of establishing my business and being rejected by the banks, my husband and I decided to obtain a second mortgage on our home. That is how we were able to establish the business and get things off the ground. Once we had the money, my second stop was to the local Small Business Administration where I received assistance in putting my business plan together. With my documentation and plans in hand, I started looking for a place to rent in order to operate the business and found a 4,000 square foot building in Hayward. I further researched what type of business I wanted to operate and decided to focus my services on new mothers and their babies; a clothing boutique for preemie babies up to young people 18 years of age.

I purchased breast pumps and bath and body products. I also obtained a permit to offer massage therapy to new moms and the general public. I flew to Florida and purchased $10,000 of babies and children's clothing from a manufacturer. I was so excited because my dream had now become a reality. Within a month, I was ready for the grand opening. I hired six staff members, including one administrative assistant, a receptionist, a certified massage therapist, a personal assistant and two customer service reps. The atmosphere of the store was beautiful and everyone felt at home. After being in business for about one year and a half, and doing quite well, all of a sudden business halted completely. A mere breast pump was rented out here and there. No longer were the customers coming in to buy clothing. I became puzzled.

A friend of mine introduced me over the phone to an evangelist who was also a prophetess. She prayed with me and said that I was not going to be in the store very long, God had a work for me to do in the vineyard. I was not pleased with what she had to share and rejected her words in my heart. I am not sure if it was fear of the unknown or just rebelliousness to God's plan for my life at that time. Within a few weeks, I realized the business was going nowhere and I needed to talk with God to find out what indeed was going on.

That particular Monday, I decided to go on a fast and put all of my staff members on a fast as well. The blessing was ironically, all of my staff were Christians so there was no conflict of interest. I needed to hear from God and I wanted all the help I could get to push my prayers through. We fasted for one week and did a lot of praying in the building, after all, we were not selling any products so our time was put to good use.

On the last day of the fast, I recall standing in the boutique section of the building amidst all the beautiful children's clothing and looking out of the window. As I meditated on God, I heard the

words, "Sharon the clothes don't bring Me Glory, the people will."
Wow! What a profound statement. I remember repeating the phrase
out loud and asking God for clarity. He did not respond. I stood in
that place for about 30 minutes just focusing my thoughts on God
hoping He would give further revelation, but to my disappointment,
He did not answer at that time. I now realize that in God's own way
and time, He will give full revelation as to what His will and purpose
is for my life.

Within a few weeks, I contracted my services with Alameda
County as a lactation consultant and a parenting educator. I began
seeing clients in the community as I received the referrals. At the
same time, I relocated to a smaller 1,200 square foot building. I
downsized my product offerings but kept all of my services including
the pump rental stations. The business began to grow again and I
was contacted by different agencies to talk about breastfeeding and
to teach women how to effectively feed their babies. It seemed as if
I was on a mission from God and didn't even realize it. The calls for
my services came seemingly out of the woodwork. One day my
personal assistant said that my "gift of gab" was where I would
receive my blessing. I remember looking at her and laughing to
myself. She was right.

Within another year, I contracted with Alameda Alliance and
was invited all over California to speak to organizations and
audiences about breastfeeding. The impact my speaking had on
people was mind boggling. I didn't correlate how what I was saying
impacted people in such an impressive way, but the words that God
revealed to me on that Monday as I stood in the boutique came back
forcefully and I understood exactly what God was trying to tell me.
Time would indeed bring the complete revelation of what God had in
store for my life.

My husband was doing well and bringing home the money.
All of our needs were met, but why was I feeling so empty, and
incomplete? I tried to ignore my feelings until one day it hit me like
a ton of bricks. The yearning to meet my biological father

resurfaced. The loneliness and void was so strong that I broke down and began to cry.

The first thing I did was to reconnect with my Uncle Baz in New York just to see if he would revisit the possibility of speaking with Earl again, hoping this time he would be willing to meet with me. Secretly, I wanted to keep my promise of settling a score with him. My family told me that on the day of my birth, Earl came by the house to see me. He gave Miss G a coin equivalent to twenty-five cents. I was determined to settle the score. I was determined to never "owe my father a cent".

The second step for me was to contact Father to let him know what I was doing and receive his blessing. After sharing my intentions with my father and receiving his blessing, I was now ready to go forward. That was all I needed in order to make it happen. I looked back in time and realized this moment was the time for me to meet him and bring closure into my life. Uncle Baz called me and said Earl had finally agreed to meet me. I arranged to fly to New York. Ironically he was living in Newburgh, New York and had been there since the mid-1960's.

I called Aunt Marie who was also living in New York and asked her to accompany me. With pleasure, she agreed. I caught a flight to New York City within the week, and after renting a car, drove to the Bronx where I reunited with Uncle Baz and Aunt Marie. Both of them were going with me to Newburgh. Once I arrived at my aunt's house, we ate a snack and then begun our three-hour drive to Newburgh.

My uncle decided to drive and I appreciated this because I needed the time to meditate on what was about to take place in my life. The drive seemed like it lasted a lifetime. Three hours seemed to turn into seven. For the entire trip, I rehearsed my words in my mind. I even tried to practice the tone of voice I was planning to use. I chuckled to myself as I pictured his expression and hoped things went exactly as I had planned. As we entered Newburgh, my uncle informed me he would be dropping us off at a gas station. He instructed us to wait at the station until he returned with Earl.

After my uncle drove away, I asked Aunt Marie some questions about what was going to happen. What if Earl didn't like me? What if he was disappointed with me for finding him and disrupting his life? What if he didn't like the way I looked? I could not stop talking. I kept asking her question after question and she did her best to appease me and keep me distracted. I was very nervous. I felt as if I waited for about two hours when in reality it had only been fifteen minutes.

Soon we saw the car coming around the corner of the gas station towards us. As the car came closer, I saw an anxious look on my uncle's face. I looked over to the man sitting next to him and saw the outline of an old, rough, dark, burly-looking man. All of a sudden, feelings of disappointment and sadness overwhelmed me. All of my emotions came to a central point. I was confused and experienced mixed emotions. I felt excited, angry, anxious, happy, sad, and helpless; all at the same time.

As my aunt and I got back into the car, Uncle Baz introduced the two of us as friends of his. My hands became clammy and sweaty. My tongue felt heavy in the roof of my mouth, as if it weighed about fifty pounds. My mind was racing at 100 miles per hour. My heart was racing at what seemed to be 1,000 beats per second, and I did not know what to do. He turned around and greeted us with a flirtatious gesture. We responded in a cordial manner.

For about two minutes into the ride, no conversation took place, only utter silence. Not even the radio was playing. I heard my uncle clear his throat and then he announced he was hungry. He asked Earl if he was hungry. He responded yes, adding he had just come from work and if he had known that there would be guests, he would have prepared himself a little better. Within minutes, we pulled up to a steak house restaurant. As we went through the line, I told my aunt and uncle that I would pay for everyone's dinner, and they accepted the offer.

We all ordered our meals and I proceeded to pay the cashier. While selecting our food from the buffet line, Earl began complaining about how little the portion of food was on his plate. The thought came to me that I should buy him another meal. I discreetly went back to the beginning of the buffet line, ordered another steak dinner and had it delivered to the table for Earl. He did not even notice what I had done. He simply thought someone was being nice to him.

We ate our meals with very little exchange of conversation. After completing his dinner, Earl leaned back in his chair as he rubbed his stomach, belched and said he was full and satisfied. We finally left the restaurant, proceeded to the car and started on the next step of our adventure. About a mile or so into our journey, Uncle Baz cleared his throat and started to speak to Earl who was in the front seat beside him. He said, "Earl, earlier today I introduced these two young ladies to you as my friends. But the truth of the matter is the young lady on the left behind me is my sister. The young lady on the right behind you is my niece, who is my sister's child, who is your child."

My world and perhaps everyone else's in the car stood still for about five seconds. Earl turned around and looked into my eyes again. This time his stare was not one of flirtation but shock. He asked me how I was doing, and kept repeating my name over and over again, "Sharon, Sharon. Oh! Sharon." Uncle Baz pulled over to the side of the road and Earl and I stepped out of the car. I remembered that I had planned to pay back my twenty-five cent debt to him first. How was I going to do that?

I opened my mouth to speak and the first thing that came out of my mouth was "Where have you been?" Then I lost it. I completely forgot about everything at that moment and the next thing I knew, I was crying like a newborn baby. He reached for me, took me in his arms, held me close and kept on repeating my name. He held me until I had calmed myself down a little bit. The void and darkness that I had felt all those years in the deepest part of my heart seemed to vanish for a few moments and I felt complete. I felt like I had finally found myself. I did not feel empty and alone now. I felt whole.

I looked intently into his face, searching for a resemblance. Maybe I had his eyes or his nose. I looked deeply but I could not see myself in him. I felt for a moment that maybe this was all a dream. In my heart, I knew this was my father and I was content with the feelings I was experiencing. We talked for about sixty minutes. I asked him to tell me his side of the story and he did. He told me he loved my mother and wanted to marry her but her father forbade him to do so.

He told me that he had two other children by another woman. They were my brothers. One was named Devon and the other was Arthur. Arthur was three months older than me and Devon was two years older. I was in shock but excited. He said my brothers were still in Jamaica as far as he knew. Unfortunately, he had not spoken to them since he left Jamaica in the sixties. After sharing other details about our lives, it was time to leave. We realized our meeting was about to be over. It was time for us to go our separate ways. Before saying good-bye, we embraced again and promised to keep in touch.

In the last few moments of our embrace, I squeezed him as tight as I could and then I finally let go. I completely forgot about the 25 cents. Instead, I gave him an 8x10 and a 5x7 picture of my family. We embraced one last time and then bid each other good-bye. When I got back into the car, a sea of emotions overwhelmed me.

I cried uncontrollably for about two hours out of the three-hour ride. Aunt Marie held my hand and consoled me while I processed and embraced my emotions. The next day after a good night's sleep, I meditated on the past day's experience and felt good about myself. I knew I had done the right thing. Once I returned home to California I called my parents in Africa and told them how much I loved them and thanked them for what they had done for me.

Chapter 14

*E*arl and I kept in touch with each other regularly. The correspondence was quite frequent, and we made plans to meet again in order for him to meet the rest of my family, which included his grandkids and my husband. I was also experiencing healing in my life. I kept my faith and relationship strong with God and my family. Some days there were negative feelings that came into my thoughts, but I was able to talk about it with my husband, and I also kept journals. I developed confidence and trust in God as He helped me become the total woman I needed to be. After all, I finally felt complete. I finally began to realize I no longer had a reason to be afraid. The more I looked at myself, the clearer God allowed me to see that I was truly "fearfully and wonderfully made" (Psalm 139:14).

I finally started to embrace who I was. I realized that I was talented and gifted. God created me and allowed me to endure all of the negative experiences for such a time as this. The more I shared my life experiences with my husband, I realized God was healing my broken heart. I focused back onto my music and as God provided opportunities to share my testimony with people I had never met before, I realized how strong I really was and embraced what God had given to me. God blessed us with two additional children, both boys. Wow, did I have my hands full. I left my job and decided to be a full-time, stay-at-home mom to my children.

After giving birth to my two youngest children, Earl and I lost contact with each other. In 1998, I wrote him three letters, however, he did not respond to any of them. I was not sure why he had not written back and decided to just let things remain dormant.

Four years later, on the seventeenth day of April, about 7:30am, my doorbell rang. We were all still asleep. The sound startled me and I rushed to answer it before it could awaken anyone else.

When I opened the front door, two police officers were standing there. They apologized for the intrusion and further explained they had received a call from someone in New York who said I needed to call my sister because there was some bad news. First of all, I did not have a sister in New York. Secondly, the only sister I had on the east coast was my guardian sister and she lived in New Jersey. I argued with the officers and told them that they had the wrong person. They asked my name and I told them Sharon. They stated they were looking for me and needed me to call the number in New York.

After no resolution to the issue, I took the number from the officers and proceeded to call. Once I dialed the number, the phone rang three times and then I heard a female voice on the other end. She asked if I was Sharon and further explained she had some bad news to share. She was sorry to tell me that my father Earl had passed away two days earlier of a massive heart attack.

I dropped the telephone and screamed at the top of my lungs. "NO, NO, NO!" I felt a flood of tears burst from a fountain within the depths of my soul. I tried to stop the tears, but they came from a place deep within me and I had no control over them. I had never experienced emotions like these before. My body began to shake uncontrollably and my mind went into instant shock. After a few moments, I regained my composure as I picked the telephone up off the floor and continued talking to the person on the other end.

The woman apologized for telling the police officers that she was my sister, but they would not give her any information about me until she identified herself as such. She told me that Earl had suffered a stroke initially. While being transported in the ambulance, the medical staff attempted to bring him back. He regained consciousness briefly, but then suffered a massive heart attack and died. I needed to get to New York. I needed to be with him. My body felt numb and my mind was blank. I could not think. I forgot where I was and what I was doing. I asked the woman where his body was being kept, and she said he was at the morgue. She was able to claim his body, but she could not make any other arrangements without my consent. I thanked her for all that she had done and asked for directions to her house. I told her that I would be in New York the following morning.

By the time I completed my conversation and hung up the telephone, my husband had come into the kitchen where I was sitting in shock. He asked what had just happened. I told him about the passing of my father Earl. He hugged me and told me he was sorry. I cried in my husband's arms for a good fifteen minutes before I was able to collect my thoughts.

I needed to make arrangements. I needed to talk to Uncle Baz and Aunt Marie. I called my uncle and told him of my father's passing. He gave me his condolences and said he would meet me in New York to help with the funeral arrangements.

Once I arrived in New York, I again rented a car and made the journey to my Aunt Marie's house. She prepared food for us and we were able to eat before making the journey back to Newburgh. This time, instead of dropping me off at the gas station, my uncle took me straight to the morgue to see my father.

Once we arrived, we sat down with the mortician to discuss the particulars of my father's passing and his arrangements. The mortician informed me he had known my father since the 1960's and they were close friends. He mentioned that my father was well known and well loved by the community.

Sadly, Earl had lived his last few years in utter poverty and isolation. He lost his job two years earlier and had just given up on life. His home was foreclosed by the bank and left abandoned. His electricity had been turned off, and there was neither heat nor water. He remained living in his own house but with no furniture or utilities. That explained why he had not responded to any more of my letters.

I am convinced he died of a broken heart and the very thought made me sad. I asked the mortician to take me to his body and he brought me into a room a little bit bigger than a broom closet. The dimly lit room terrified me. I entered the room ahead of my uncle and wished I could turn around and walk out, but it was too late. As I walked around to the side of the body, I viewed a naked man laying on a slab with his head propped on a neck stand.

I saw someone I did not recognize. He looked somewhat like the man I had seen a few years earlier. He was the same height and the same complexion. I could not recognize my father. His face was twisted and there was still blood on the corner of his mouth. I looked at my uncle and he acknowledged that this indeed was my father Earl. I needed to get out of that room as soon as possible.

We went back into the mortician's office to discuss the financial concerns. He informed me that my father had an insurance policy of seventy thousand dollars. All I needed to do was go to the bank and I would be able to sign and get the funds to take care of the burial.

I left the mortuary and proceeded to the bank where I learned my father had only 95 cents in the bank. I then went to his former job and was told that two years prior he was injured. He went out on disability and shortly thereafter, was laid off. He was unable to return to work and had ultimately lost his job. He gave up on life, himself, and everything around him.

I was heartbroken. I returned to the mortuary and proceeded to arrange for the funeral and pay for the entire affair. My father Earl had died as a pauper, but I was determined to bury him as a king with pride and dignity. I gave him the best funeral a person could have wished for. I chose a bronze casket with gold trimming and had him dressed in a beautiful brown pinstriped suit.

His friends and associates from the community came to the funeral. Over 100 people showed up. I even asked Father to perform the funeral, and he did, with pride. He did not even know Earl, but he chose to do the funeral for my sake.

While making funeral arrangements, I tried desperately to locate my two brothers and was unsuccessful in finding them. I sent a telegram to Jamaica but they did not receive it until after his burial.

After the funeral, I returned to California and tried to put the pieces of my life back together again. About three months after the funeral, I received a call from a man in Jamaica. He asked if I was Sharon. I responded with a hesitant yes. He then informed me that he was my brother. He heard his father had passed away. I told him yes and that I was sorry. I asked him how he had gotten my telephone number and he said it was on a telegram he received from the post office that was three months old.

We talked for about fifty minutes and then ended the conversation. Before saying goodbye, we promised to see each other soon. I made up my mind to take a trip to Jamaica within the next month. I was so excited. I planned to spend two weeks on the Island with my brothers. In between the time for me to go to Jamaica, my brother and I spoke at least four times a week for at least fifteen minutes per call. We had so much to discuss. Each time we talked, we learned so much more about each other.

The day finally arrived for the trip to Jamaica to meet my brothers. As I boarded the airplane in Los Angeles, the excitement that bubbled up inside of me was unbearable. I could not wait to touch down at the Montego Bay airport. As we circled the airport in preparation for landing, the tears began to flow down my face.

The thought came to my mind that out of death comes life. If my father had not died, perhaps I would not have had this once in a lifetime opportunity to meet my brothers. The airplane landed and I heard the sound of that old rickety staircase being pushed to the side of the plane in order for us to disembark. I could not wait to go inside the terminal. The airport looked so different from the day I first left Jamaica. I located my luggage and after clearing customs, I exited the terminal.

I searched through the crowd of people for someone who looked like my father, and to my pleasant surprise, I spotted my brother at the same time he spotted me. We ran towards each other and embraced. We held each other for a good five minutes as we shed tears of joy together. The feelings that rushed into my heart, soul and mind were indescribable. We were happy beyond words. I lost my father but I found my brother Arthur. Even though he was three months older than I, we shared many similarities as if we were twins.

Life meant everything to me at this moment. Arthur told me that my older brother Devon was at home anxiously waiting for our return. The drive from the airport to Savanna-la-Mar was three hours. The time allowed us to talk about everything under the sun. I learned so much about my brother. In addition, he learned plenty about me. My brother Arthur had two children, a girl, and a boy. Arthur's son was seven and his daughter was sixteen. I was an aunt and I could not believe it.

As we entered the yard of Arthur's house, I saw a beautiful two-story home. I spotted some people peeping out of the second story apartment and knew it was my brother Devon and his family. As we parked the car and climbed the stairs to the house, everyone came outside on the balcony to meet us. We all embraced each other and I settled into my room to talk with my brothers.

We embraced once more and then began to talk about our father. My two brothers and I cried together as a family. We shared the fact that if our father had not passed away, we would not have met each other. We were grateful to our father for the sacrifice he made for us. We felt even though he did not have the opportunity to reunite with his three children, he had given of himself in order for us to be together as a family.

I spent those two weeks with my brother Arthur. The first morning, after a peaceful night's rest, I awoke to him playing a tune on the keyboard. What I heard coming from my brother shocked me. Arthur's voice was as smooth as butter. He sang in a cool high tenor tone and I was astonished and impressed all at the same time.

Not only did my brother play the piano, he also played the bass guitar and the drums. I realized how much we had in common, Even thou we were two months apart, we shared so many common traits as if we were actually twins. We were both vocally gifted and musically inclined. Wow! Every morning upon waking up, we had a jam session at the piano where we performed countless duets, solos and instrumental renditions for each other. So much joy and music resonated throughout my brother's home for duration of my visit.

My oldest brother Devon was also a gifted furniture maker. I was amazed at his finesse and attention to detail as he created beds, bed heads, dressing tables and other pieces of furniture. Our father truly had three uniquely talented and gifted children and we were mighty proud.

Each and every day of the trip was spent touring and sightseeing many of the attractions in Jamaica as well as the places of my childhood. We spent a couple days visiting the beaches of Negril. During my visit, Arthur took me to my great grandmother's gravesite outside of Savanna-la-Mar, and to my grandfather's grave in Darliston. We also went to the gravesite of Earl's mother, our grandmother. I remember standing upon the grave of my grandfather and the tears rose up within my heart. I knew that I had made full circle in my life in more ways than one. I was so excited for the experience.

Within six months Arthur, my twin as I call him, made the voyage to California to meet my family. The trip was twofold because he and I were also flying to New York so I could take him to the place where his father had been laid to rest, and he could find peace and closure.

Before we made our way to the cemetery, I took him to the house where our father lived and we were both shocked and outraged by what we saw. The street our father lived on was cobblestone. It was said that Newburgh was about 100 years old; low income and poor migrant families from the West Indies and other countries now inhabited the town.

As we walked down the street to the house where our father lived, we were constantly stepping over discarded needles and other drug paraphernalia. Candles, dried flowers, and old stuffed animals left a neglected shrine on the front porch. We took many pictures and said our good-byes to the past as we made our way to the cemetery.

Once we found the plot, my brother stood on his father's grave and I made my way back to the car to give him privacy. I saw his mouth move and knew he was talking with his dad. I do not know what he said and I chose not to ask him. I felt it was very private and sacred between my brother and his father. After about twenty minutes, my brother made his way back to the car and sat down in the passenger's seat. As he sat down, my brother broke down and cried. I took his hand and comforted him. His tears were of sadness and joy at the same time. I felt his pain and his brokenness because we shared the same emotions. We left the cemetery and made a vow to embrace the future while keeping our father's memory alive in our hearts and minds. Upon his return to Jamaica we vowed to keep in touch and visit each other on a regular basis, at least once per year.

After Earl's death and meeting my brothers for the first time, I decided to go back to college. I earned my bachelor's degree with a BA in Maternal Child Health, and worked as an International Board Certified Lactation Consultant in private practice. The experience I gained helped me to start my own business.

I opened a consulting firm where my staff and I worked with women from all over Alameda County who struggled with their infants. I also taught parenting classes for the county and worked with hundreds of hurting men, women and teens who have experienced abuse or were emotionally traumatized as children.

The following year, in 2004, Father's brother passed away. While in Jamaica for the funeral, my cousin, who was my uncle's only child, asked me to sing at the service. It began at 9:00 in the morning and did not conclude until about 3:30 in the afternoon. It was not a day of mourning, but a day of celebration and rejoicing.

When called upon, I sang "I Won't Complain" to a standing ovation. After completing it, the pastor called me up to sing another song. I ended up singing three songs during the whole service. The pastor rose to his feet and stood in front of the congregation. He looked over at his choir and then looked back at me. With an astonished expression, he boldly proclaimed in his strong Jamaican accent "Is a shame, ah one ah she an ah fifty ah hoonoo and she hout sing hall ah hoonoo!" Laughter broke out across the congregation. I was so embarrassed for the choir and for myself. What I did not realize was that day birthed the confirmation of my musical journey.

After the burial, my cousin and I were on the outside of the church talking amongst ourselves when the pastor approached us. We acknowledged him and he began to speak some powerful statements into my life.

He said, "Sister Sharon, God said to tell you that He has given you a gift and you are not using it for His honor and His Glory. If you don't begin to use your musical talents, specifically your voice to bring others to Christ, God will take your singing gift". He went on to say that I should not have been struggling for all those years. He continued that once I decided to use my singing to share with the world, then I would begin to see a change in my life and circumstances.

I remember looking at the pastor and thinking he did not know anything about me. It was shocking to see how God used him to speak to me. The next day I was invited to sing at a youth convention, but I declined since I was preparing to return home.

As I think back to this part of my journey, I am moved by the Spirit of God. On the flight back to the United States, I remember looking out of the window as the sun was beginning to set in the distance. The blue sky was changing to a faint grey color. The cotton ball clouds were floating gently beneath the airplane and the words of the pastor returned to the forefront of my mind.

I released my mind and thoughts towards God and the Lord spoke to me saying, "Sharon, it is the anointing that makes the difference in your life". That is where I wrote the very first song for my *Miracle's* CD.

During that six-hour flight from Montego Bay to Los Angeles, seventeen songs and their melodies were birthed into my spirit and mind, one after the other like a waterfall flowing gently over smooth rocks. I wrote, cried, sang, laughed and wrote the music. I could not wait to get home to share my revelation and songs with my husband and family. The connecting flight could not leave Los Angeles and arrive in San Francisco fast enough for me to get to work on my music.

I found a new burst of energy. The music mattered to me and I was excited. I was on my journey and it felt right. As my husband picked me up from the airport, I shared my experience and asked him to purchase a new keyboard for me. The next day my husband took me to the music store and purchased a top of the line Yamaha keyboard. I couldn't wait to get home and release the tunes out of my heart and into my mouth and fingers.

I sang the seventeen songs for my husband and children and they were excited for me. I then recorded the songs on a tape recorder and made a call to my father in Connecticut asking if he knew of a pianist or producer who could help with my project. He recommended my little brother named "Donavon" who began as the organist for his church. Donavon had graduated from college and relocated to Los Angeles to pursue his destiny in the music/producing world.

I contacted Donavon and within a couple of weeks, was on a flight to Los Angeles to go record in the studio with him. I knew nothing about the music industry. Thankfully Donovan taught me the foundations of what I needed to succeed.

The process began and I was well on my way. Our studio was his bedroom full of keyboards, microphones and wires. My sound booth was his clothes closet. I would sing, one song, Donavon would play the music and then had me take a walk for a couple of hours so he could arrange the music. We did this for two days and the only break we took was to use the bathroom and put food in our stomachs.

By the end of the weekend, we completed six out of the 17 songs and planned for the next opportunity for me to come back to Los Angeles and record some more. I was able to pay Donavon a couple of hundred dollars for his work. While helping with my CD, he was also working on his own music and continuing towards his goal of becoming a producer/artist.

I made one more trip to Los Angeles within a few months and we did what was necessary to set the foundation. Donavon and I were our own background singers along with my sister-friend Esther, whom accompanied me on the second trip.

Not long after my two trips to Los Angeles, it was time for me to return to Jamaica for another visit with my brothers. This time, I decided to take two of my three sons, Donovan Jr. and David.

All this time, the words which the pastor had spoken to me at the funeral were in the back of my mind. I sensed that God was birthing a new thing in me, but I was only experiencing pieces at a time. He was leading and directing my path. Everything which took place was according to the will and plan of God for my life. The end result would be revealed at a later time.

It was now the summer of 2005 and this trip was exciting, because Arthur took the boys and I to many attractions including the beach. We had a lot of fun. On one particular day we planned to go to the beach and were excited about the day unfolding. As we began our journey, my brother announced we were making a quick stop on the way because he wanted to introduce me to one of his friends named Patrick. I was a bit perturbed because I did not feel like making any stops anywhere to meet anyone, failing to realize that God had ordained this meeting.

As we pulled up to the front lawn of Patrick's home, I heard the most beautiful music resounding from the window. I became intrigued and asked my brother who this Patrick was. Arthur responded that Patrick was one of the top producers and keyboardists in the Island of Jamaica. Uh oh! What was about to happen?

As we approached the front of the house, my brother rang the door bell and a gentleman opened the door. Music was ringing throughout the entire house. We entered and my brother introduced us to Patrick. Arthur told Patrick that I was a gospel singer from America and he wanted us to meet. Patrick was excited about meeting me and asked me to sing something. I was so embarrassed because I was dressed and ready to go to the beach, not to sing, but my focus shifted quickly from the beach to the music.

Patrick pulled out an older model keyboard and plugged it in. He asked me to sing again. I began singing "Your Grace and Mercy". Patrick was so shocked, he asked me to sing another song. The thought came to my mind that I could ask if Patrick would assist in taking my CD to the next level. He agreed and after spending three hours singing my brother ending up taking my two boys to the beach without me. Patrick arranged for a keyboard player to come the next day. We would sing the lead vocals and he would arrange the rest of the music while I went back to the States.

I returned to Patrick's home the next day and he'd brought in a pianist named Dwayne to play for me. I sang six songs into the microphone while Dwayne played for about four hours and Patrick recorded and rerecorded. When I returned home to California Patrick was able to solicit the assistance of some of Jamaica's great musicians who took time in between their touring schedule to go into the studio and add the music to my voice.

About six months after my initial recordings with Patrick, I returned to Jamaica and was pleasantly surprised by the production of the music. I remember being moved to tears from the awesomeness of God and how He does things in our lives. The seed had been planted and continued to grow in Jamaica.

During my visit in the spring of 2006, Patrick reserved time at a studio in Negril for us to add the background vocals. I met with the owner of the studio and after a brief conversation, we proceeded with the recording. As I looked around the room, I counted six background singers; two sopranos, two tenors and two alto voices. It was my job to teach their parts for the first song. I overheard one of the sound engineers saying, "Wow, what a woman. Not only is she the lead vocalist, imagine she has to play a dual role of teaching everyone their parts at the same time, amazing!"

The group finally learned their parts and it was now time to record. I was anxious for this part of the process to be completed. Since I was so green at the recording experience, I never thought twice about the suggestion of recording all the voice parts at the same time. Everything sounded good while the group was singing, but when it was time to replay the recording, my goodness, things sounded imbalanced. Some of the voices could be heard out-singing others and it was as if everyone was in a competition.

We continued on with the second, third, fourth, fifth and finally the sixth song. By then everyone had been singing consistently for about 18 hours. Nightfall had come and all of us had reached utter exhaustion. We rapped up the session and then it was time to say good-bye to the background singers, allowing the sound engineer to create his magic by mixing the voices with the music. I decided to stay at the studio. Brother Elliot, one of my new faithful fans who had begun the trip with me from Patrick's home in Savanna-la-Mar, decided to remain at the studio with me throughout the night to lend moral support.

The lack of sleep attacked my body from every angle. I would sit for a while, and then walk for a while in order to stay awake. This night was long, and seemed never ending. As daybreak cracked the sky, the engineer completed all of his work. I was relieved and ready to let out a big scream. It had been a very long and arduous process, but I learned so much and now as I look back, I thank God for the experience.

After the music was mixed and copied onto a CD later that morning, it was finally time for me to head back to Arthur's house. The next day I boarded the plane for my journey home with my CD, audio tape and copies in hand. Based on what I'd heard in the studio, I felt it was ready to be mastered, then enabling me to simply replicate and distribute for the world to hear.

I finally made my way back to San Francisco and upon arrival, I mailed a copy of the CD to my brother-friend/manager so he could hear the music and give either his blessing or disapproval. Once Leonard received his copy, he called me and I held my breath for his response.

He began by saying, "My sister, you know that I respect you. What I am going to say is not to hurt you. The music compilation is beautiful, however, the mixing and voices and so on is not good!" My heart seemed to drop from my chest cavity to the bottom of my stomach. I was so disappointed with his verdict. Leonard further stated that for the caliber of music I wrote, I deserved better and he felt it needed to be redone.

I wanted to cry. I felt stuck and wondered where was I going to find the funds to continue paying for this project, after spending a couple thousand of dollars so far. I decided to put every thing on hold until I could collect my thoughts and decide what the next step would be.

After a few months, I picked up the project again and decided to pursue my options as to what it would take to get it completed. After consulting with a couple producers who heard my CD, the final recommendation was to re-do the entire project including the background music and mixing process. The price quotes I received were discouraging my spirit more and more, but I never had the inclination to give up. I simply believed in my music and was determined to see it through to the end.

A few more months passed by and I was invited to sing in a gospel concert in Connecticut. I gladly participated but resented the fact that all of the other artists had products to share with the audience, and I had nothing. I was disappointed, but never let go of my dreams. I believed in my heart that my CD would come to fruition ultimately.

Another couple of months went by; it was now the fall of 2006. I met another producer who listened to my project and said he could re-do it if I gave him ten thousand dollars. I knew I didn't have that kind of money, so I told him that I would pray about it and see what the Lord said and then get back to him with my answer. I ended up not accepting the offer. As I look back at that period, it was not the right time for my miracle to come to pass.

Another couple of months went by and it was now the winter of 2006. At this same time, I had been working in my new job at Kaiser Hospital as a manager for over a year and was hiring people for various positions.

This is how my "Miracle" began with my CD. Just to go back in time a little bit, in June 2005, my third child David had to undergo surgery for his spine. Since I was the Music Director at my church, it was necessary for me to find a substitute to replace me while on medical leave with my son. A young lady had visited my church occasionally; she was an organist who was not playing full-time for any church at the time. I contacted her and asked if she would mind replacing me temporarily while I cared for my son. With pleasure she agreed and after receiving my Senior Pastor's approval, she began to play for our church. A few months later she asked if the hospital was hiring. After checking the availability of job opportunities, I informed her that there were openings and she should apply. Ultimately, she was able to obtain employment and was grateful for the opportunity. As time progressed, she ended up in my department.

One day out of no where, I blurted, "I need my CD to be completed. Do you know anyone who can help me?" This was about March of 2007. All of a sudden, she jumped up out of her chair and proclaimed, "That's it!" She pulled out her cell phone and made a call to a producer friend of hers who lived in Atlanta. After speaking with the young man for a brief moment, she told him that she needed a favor; she had someone who needed a CD completed. She was tired of hearing me cry about it and wanted to know if he could help. He asked her what I could afford.

At that moment, I did not even have the fifty cents to mail the CD to Atlanta. She told him, "She can only afford one dollar". He laughed and then we all broke out into laughter. He thought for a moment and asked her if I could afford five thousand dollars. I thought for a moment. Extending my faith towards God, I looked at her and said, "Yes, tell him yes!"

It was time for us to move forward. By that weekend, I mailed the CD to Atlanta. Within a couple of months, he had completely rearranged the music, separated the voices and asked me to fly to Atlanta to re-do the lead vocals. Not only did he rearrange the music, he also added new background vocals. What I heard totally blew my mind. I remember hearing the music for the first time and breaking into tears because I could not believe the prophecy which had been given to me a couple of years earlier was finally coming to pass.

I spent one week in Atlanta, singing in the studio from 9:00 each morning and ending about midnight each night, Monday through Thursday. By Thursday, we had completed all eleven songs which were going to be on the album. It was time for the CD to be mixed and mastered.

Upon returning to San Francisco, I was introduced to Carl the Mixer who is one of the best producers in the Bay Area. Carl received my package from the producer in Atlanta. One more step to go. He invited me to his studio so we could hear the music together.

After our initial greeting, we both sat in the booth and he pushed a button. Nothing would play. I became concerned. I could not believe that I had come this far only for my music to not play as it should. Following repeated attempts to reload the music, Carl determined the drive it was recorded on was not the best. He needed the producer in Atlanta to resend the music to him again. A week later, Carl was in Atlanta for a show. He went to the producer's home, copied the music on a different drive and brought it back to his studio in San Francisco.

I began to see the light at the end of the tunnel. Carl began his magic of mixing the music. I received a phone call one day and it was bad news. Some of the music had been infected, which meant he could not use it. He ended up having to re-do the music which meant further delay. Again, I found myself swallowing my saliva and saying, "Lord, how long?" I made up my mind that I had come too far to give up now. No matter how long it took, I knew everything was going to be alright. Within a couple of weeks, Carl had remedied all of the imperfections, added music and used other musicians to enhance the project. We were on our way to completion.

I sent another copy to my brother-friend, Leonard. When he called me this time, he was so moved with emotion. I ended up laughing at him inside myself and also crying with joy because I had finally passed the test.

I now understand clearly that God created me to be exactly who I am today. I am a strong woman. I am a self-assured wife and mother and I was created to be a light to many dark and broken hearts across the world. I am becoming a world-renowned author and lecturer. I am an anointed Psalmist/Gospel Artist and I am a motivational speaker and an international licensed evangelist with my church. I returned to school to complete my double master's degree in counseling psychology and forensic psychology with a certification in pastoral counseling. I desire to become a licensed marriage and family therapist, enabling me to have my practice on a part-time basis while ministering globally in both in song and spoken word. If I choose to continue in my educational pursuits, I will eventually become a licensed psychologist. Only time will tell.

I am a blessed woman of God to be able to travel the world sharing my journey and the secret to "complete success". I share my story of how I learned to pick up the pieces of my broken life and turned them over to God, who put them back together and made me whole. I am grateful for my experiences. I am humbled that God created me to go through all of the trials in my life, because through them I am now able to help others turn their lives around.

One sunny afternoon while standing in my kitchen washing dishes, I looked out the window into the sky. I realized it was a beautiful and peaceful day. The sky was blue and those snow-white cotton ball clouds were slowly passing by, while the sun peeked through on the sides.

I smiled to myself as the clouds seemed to say to me, "Remember we said you were going to begin your life anew? Remember we told you that we would never leave you or forsake you? In addition, remember we told you that we would always be with you and protect you for the rest of your life?"

Just as God had been with the children of Israel during their journey out of Egypt through the wilderness into Canaan land, where He protected them with a cloud by day and a pillar of fire by night, God has been with me from my mother's womb until this very day.

I nodded, as the salty tears rolled down both sides of my cheeks, meeting at the center of my chin. I realized those same snow-white cotton ball clouds were God's way of visibly showing me that He was always with me, to comfort and encourage me. I thought to myself, how blessed I was to have found it in the clouds.

End Note

Jones' ultimate goals are: become a best-selling non-fiction author, a multi-platinum gospel artist, operate a part-time private practice as a Clinical Psychologist and be a quintessential role model for women and youth from all lifestyles.

Sharon is an anointed woman of God who ministers from her heart. She writes, speaks and sings from her soul and her gift is evident through her music, lyrics and in her ministering. Her Jamaican-American music style is unique, fresh and on the cutting edge.

Sharon's first solo project began with her single release titled "I Won't Complain", published by Pure One Publishing. She is following up with a full compilation project titled "Miracles", to be released in September 2007.

For booking or more information, contact:

CELL 510-754-0661
E-MAIL SHADOJE@AOL.COM OR SHARONM.JONES@YAHOO.COM

WWW.SMJHEALINGMYHEARTMINISTRY.COM

www.ingramcontent.com/pod-product-compliance
Lightning Source LLC
Chambersburg PA
CBHW072012040426
42447CB00009B/1598